S0-BXZ-955

Pale Morning Dun

Pale Morning Dun

Stories by
Richard Dokey

University of Missouri Press
Columbia and London

Copyright © 2004 by Richard Dokey
University of Missouri Press, Columbia, Missouri 65201
Printed and bound in the United States of America
All rights reserved
5 4 3 2 1   08 07 06 05 04

Library of Congress Cataloging-in-Publication Data

Dokey, Richard.
  Pale morning dun : stories / by Richard Dokey.
    p. cm.
  ISBN 0-8262-1511-4 (alk. paper)
  I. Title.
PS3554.O42P35   2004
813'.54—dc22   2003022909

♾ This paper meets the requirements of the
American National Standard for Permanence of Paper
for Printed Library Materials, Z39.48, 1984.

Designer: Jennifer Cropp
Typesetter: Crane Composition, Inc.
Printer and binder: The Maple-Vail Book Manufacturing Group
Typefaces: Aquinas and Minion

The following stories, often in somewhat different form, originally
appeared in these periodicals:

"Hampstead's Folly," *Clockwatch Review;* "The Beggar of Union Square,"
Literary Review; "The Monster" and "Never Trust the Weatherman,"
Chariton Review; "Pale Morning Dun" and "The Shopper," *Missouri
Review;* "A House in Order," *Writers' Forum;* "The Suicide," *Interim;*
"Monkey," *Confrontation;* "Vital Statistics," *TriQuarterly;* "The Electric
Dog," *Washington Review;* "Ace," *Laurel Review;* "The Mouse," *Flyway.*

PUBLICATION OF THIS BOOK HAS BEEN ASSISTED
BY THE WILLIAM PEDEN MEMORIAL FUND

In Memory Of
JOHN R. MILTON
Editor and Friend

Contents

Pale Morning Dun

Hampstead's Folly

He was not happy, but that didn't matter. There are consolations in any life. Even a prisoner finds comfort at evening.

His name was Andrew Hampstead and he had enough money, but that didn't matter either. He had learned that from the divorce, when his wife took most of everything and left him just enough, and now enough was all he needed. She had taken the children, too, and for awhile that had pained him deeply, but he was not sure, even now, if the pain had truly been the loss of them or only the sound at dusk of empty rooms.

There is a moment when the mind decides to go no further and life becomes a parade. Andrew Hampstead had reached that moment. Events were arrivals and departures on a timetable. He made stops and connections. He embarked and came home. But it was all the same. The days marched by and disappeared around a corner.

He was not bitter. The things that had happened to him happened to many men. Divine providence or luck—knock on wood—had spared him the travesty of a second or third marriage. He was suspicious of emotion and convinced that people could not live together and certain that they could not live alone. So it was all folly, and he spent the days getting through and the nights in grateful repose. He liked the nights, because when he looked out his window, he could not see the world, and it did not matter that there was no place to go.

He was a creature of habit, as one who relies solely upon himself often is, but these habits were uneven and did not extend to all his life. He ironed his own shirts and groomed himself carefully, but his rooms were careless and disarrayed, and a layer of dust lay upon the end tables and dressers. There was enough futility around without adding to it, he reasoned, and the dust only returned.

One evening, while he sat under yellow lamplight reading a book, the telephone rang, and it was a policeman informing him that his ex-wife and son had been killed in a collision with a freight train, but his daughter was all right because she was at a neighbor's, and now she had given the police this number to call. He thanked the officer and went to the closet for his coat and hat.

He drove through the night and arrived at the small town upstate at three in the morning. A light was burning in the neighbor's window. He sat in the car for a moment and watched the window, and then he got out and went up to the front door.

A middle-aged woman answered his ring. She was dressed in a red terry cloth robe, and there were circles under her eyes. "Mr. Hampstead," she said with relief and some embarrassment. "Please come in. I'm Mildred Hafley."

There was a balding, heavyset man asleep in a recliner before the television. One of the man's slippers had fallen off. The woman walked hurriedly over and poked the man's stomach. He grunted and his feet jumped. The other slipper dropped to the floor.

"Ben," she said, "he's here."

The fat man struggled to his feet, rubbed his eyes, and came toward him with his hand out. "I'm awfully sorry, old man," he said, "awfully sorry."

"Thank you," Andrew said, because he could not think of anything else, and then he said, "You're kind to keep Jennifer here."

"She's a fine little girl," the man said, "a real charmer. You should be proud of her. You'll have to be careful that someone doesn't steal her away." Then he seemed to think a moment and said, "We're aw-fully sorry, you know."

"Thank you," he said.

"She's upstairs in bed," the woman said. "Would you like me to get her for you? I know you're anxious to have her. It's so terrible, Mr. Hampstead." She burst into tears.

The last time he had visited his children was three years ago, and he was not sure what the proper thing was to say. He looked about the rather conventional room, with its mirror over the fireplace, por-celain knickknacks on the mantel, and the upright piano in one cor-ner between two potted palms, and said, "May I go up and fetch her myself, please?"

"Oh, of course," she said. "That would certainly be the good thing to do."

He was glad of that and tried to smile.

"First door at the head of the stairs," the man said.

He climbed the stairs and went into the room. She was asleep on the bed with all her clothes on.

The room belonged to some other child who had grown up and gone away. There were posters on the walls and a picture of an owl-faced girl in a cap and gown standing between a man and woman. The man looked like Ben Hafley, only with hair and a flat stomach. The woman was not the woman downstairs.

He stepped closer and peered at Jennifer. He was struck by the re-semblance to her mother. There were the soft, full lashes, the curl at the edge of the mouth, the high cheekbones, and the gentle flatten-ing at the tip of the nose. Sleep did the same thing to both mother and daughter. It removed intelligence and left that quality of the feminine which some actresses of great skill can create, and then only briefly.

Tears came to his eyes and he was not sure why. He was not thinking of either his dead son or his ex-wife. It was the sleep, perhaps, and his daughter so full with it. It was that she was asleep and lovely and un-touched. He had not seen her in years and she was asleep and would awaken and everything would start and he didn't know what to do.

He held his breath, foolish and ashamed. He longed for one, just one frame to stand still in the lens of time. He coughed. His daughter opened her eyes and, seeing her father standing beside the bed, his own eyes red and glistening, she misconstrued everything and threw her arms about him, calling, "Daddy, Daddy! Oh, my daddy!"

He brought her to his rooms in the city. Immediately she set about cleaning the place. He would come home from work to find that she had dusted the furniture or vacuumed the rugs or scrubbed the sink in the bathroom. She made out lists of things for him to buy, and the towels took on a fresh scent, and there seemed always to be the odor of lemon or pine in the air, and the dishes shone.

He was pressed to find things to do. She had been taken away so long ago that he had lost the spontaneity that is necessary with the young. She was a visitor.

They went for walks in the park. They went to movies. Sometimes they drove out into the country and had picnics, and sometimes they went to the zoo and watched the animals. He took her downtown and bought her new fall clothes and a portable Sony for her bedroom. In all this there was a certain quality of arrangement, like life settling to the bottom of a bowl. He was not sure what it meant. He was not even sure that he was happy to have her with him, ironing his shirts and preparing macaroni and cheese and canned string beans when he got home from work. He knew, though, that he felt thankful when she retired to her room to watch television and left him alone under the lamp with a book.

But he did feel a strong sense of responsibility, which increased as the time drew near for her to go to school again. He realized how much he did not understand, how little prepared he was to help her, and how often the quiet settled about them, alone together beneath all that life.

He was concerned lest she think he acted toward her only out of duty. She had suffered enough, certainly, and in spite of his own case, he did not believe it wise that one should learn too young to live without hope. He wanted what was right for her, though he feared righteousness. He wanted her to be happy, though he believed it truly had nothing to do with him. He lay awake thinking about it. He had a twelve-year-old daughter on his hands and, *let's face it, you don't know what to do,* he thought, *you need someone to step in here and take this thing off your back.*

He considered a housekeeper or a governess, even a boarding school. There were people at work who sent their children away, and Milt Washburn, whose wife had died of a brain tumor two years ago, employed a woman to come in and take care of his son.

These choices troubled him. Watching Jennifer move about the boxy rooms, her thin white legs and slender arms struggling to arrange life in some order that might be called love, he felt helpless and betrayed. He had to put aside everything and, for her sake, find a reason to live.

In doing this he was not sure what his place in it all should be. The choice did not even seem logical, though there was a bizarre sense of logic about it. And as far as his own needs were concerned, whatever they were, a decision like this was irrelevant. He would simply give Jennifer a new mother.

At the office there was a Vera Mallory, secretary to Mr. Hastings, the personnel manager. She reminded him of one of those women you find pushing a shopping cart down the aisle of a supermarket at ten in the morning. She was overweight, with dimpled elbows and full calves, but she had a pretty face, a soft lower lip, and her eyes were the darkest blue he had ever seen. She should have been married all her life, planning menus and sorting clothes over a dryer, but as far as he knew, she had never even been engaged, and when the salesmen passed by and flirted with her, she lowered her eyes, blushed, and reached for a cream-filled chocolate from the box she always kept in the bottom drawer of her desk.

He liked her. There was a courtesy about her, a genuine courtesy, that he found relaxing and peaceful. He often sat beside her in the cafeteria downstairs, smelling her flowery perfume and imagining her bringing him coffee and bourbon on a rainy evening. This feeling was not one of desire. It only made the time pass more pleasantly beneath the hubbub of noise from the tables around him and the glare off the aluminum urns.

He sat next to her one day in early September, when Jennifer had started school, and tried to see the three of them at the oaken table in the living room eating roast beef. Jennifer would like Vera's large, open smile, he was sure, and her perfect teeth. She would like the friendly shyness, which, along with the courtesy, would guarantee that she would have a voice in things. He did not want a woman in the house telling his daughter what to do. He was wise enough to understand that, whatever else she was, Jennifer Hampstead only needed that soft touch of the feminine to free her from childhood.

He expected nothing for himself. It was this, after all, which made it possible for him to entertain the notion in the first place, and as he thought about it during the ensuing days, chatting with Vera a little more amiably over dessert and coffee, there was not the slightest doubt that he would succeed. He would be unambiguously kind to her. He would honor and keep her. He would place her at the very front of all his consideration and effort. He would give up for her some of his evenings alone reading. He would cherish her as one would a faithful and trusted servant who was given the run of the house. One day he might even discover a kind of affection for her, and he believed he could satisfy her.

He was not sure how to proceed. He had not been separated from Jennifer since she had joined him, and he did not want her to think that suddenly there was a part of his life he could not share. She was not an infant, and she did not need a sitter. Yet he could not leave her alone. One thing he could do was to take Vera out to lunch while he worked on the problem, and so they began going to a little Italian place around the corner. She seemed deeply appreciative, and he held her hand, which surprised him with its warmth. All he needed was one weekend, he figured, before he brought her home for dinner, and finally he hit upon a scheme.

How would she like to go visit the Hafleys?

"The Hafleys, Daddy?"

"They were such nice people. It would be a shame not to say hello once in a while."

"The Hafleys only lived next door, Daddy. And they were Mommy's friends."

"Aren't there some children your age up there that you'd like to visit again?"

"I'm making new friends here."

"I see," he said.

He sat down in the chair and turned on the yellow lamp.

"The Hafleys are all right," she said.

"I thought you might like to go back and visit for a day," he said, smiling. "I don't want you to feel cooped up here."

"I'm not," she said. "I like it here. I even like hearing the cars go by at night."

"I'm glad. I only want you to feel happy, that's all. The Hafleys said they'd be delighted to have you come and visit anytime."

The lie made his forehead damp.

"The Hafleys are all right," she said. Then she went into her bedroom and closed the door. A half hour later she returned and said, "I'll go, Daddy."

"Don't go if you don't want to, Jen. I only want to be sure that you're happy."

"I'll go. The Hafleys are nice."

"Good. I'll call them, then."

"All right," she said, and went back to her bedroom.

He explained the situation to Ben Hafley, and the following Saturday morning drove Jennifer up to spend the day. That evening he took Vera to the theater and a late supper.

The next weekend he helped his daughter prepare a special meal for a special guest, and Jennifer found herself looking over a steaming platter of roast beef at the smiling, shy, round face of a woman who smelled like a bowl of carnations.

He married her a month later. Jennifer was the flower girl. They had the ceremony in a little place that looked out on the river, and there were trees and a redwood platform on which they all stood, and a man played the guitar and sang theme songs from movies.

There couldn't be a honeymoon, at least not immediately. He

explained it to Vera, and she respected his wishes about leaving Jennifer alone. After all, she was grateful.

So they settled down in his rooms. He moved her chest of drawers next to his dresser and her two chairs opposite the sofa. They had meat loaf and baked halibut and roast beef. Vera was a fine cook, and he put on weight. They went to concerts and symphonies and sometimes to the theater. Vera helped Jennifer with homework, and Jennifer helped Vera with the dishes. He was able to sit under the lamp from time to time and read a book. Everything was as he had expected.

He came to realize very quickly how important another adult is as an intermediary. Alone with Jennifer, he had known a kind of hollowness, as though, when he spoke to her, a reverberation came from the walls, and he felt outnumbered. Now the sense that he was always doing something wrong disappeared. There was a woman in the house, and that was proper when you had a daughter. He was unburdened of a part of himself that made him uncomfortable, and Vera seemed pleased enough to take over.

So life ran smoothly, or so it seemed. He was able to adjust his routine and make new habits. Jennifer did well in school. Vera, surprisingly, was losing weight. Her face seemed to lengthen and stop being just pretty and become actually, in a way, beautiful. When they all went out together, he noticed how people looked at them, and he counted himself lucky.

But he could not overcome the years of solitude. After the divorce, when Jenny and her brother were still quite small, he had experienced a separation so intense that he imagined only prisoners in a concentration camp might understand such suffering. For those who have always had people about them, first parents and then, immediately, their own families, living suddenly alone is an abyss.

He could not bring himself to do the things that all the others did. He did not go to the places where people who are afraid of loneliness go. He would not submit to the failure to be human so that he could be human after all. There was something common in it, like something out of a magazine, and his life, to his way of thinking, was unique. He had married and fathered children, and the divorce came and took the vanity away. He sat down in his silent rooms, and the lamp above his chair was the light that illumined the universe.

So now these two others were with him and he found himself arranging them according to his privacy. There was almost a compulsion about it, since he had planned for neither of them. Though welcome to a point, they could not find the center of him, which he kept safe in the solitude of his nights.

With all things patterns develop, and as he remained close to the reading lamp, so did they draw comfort from each other. Often he would hear them laughing in the bedroom and sometimes they sang. He was glad they liked each other. He could not complain, for they never excluded him and welcomed him whenever he peeked through the door to see what all the commotion was about. Yet it never worked the other way around. When they all sat in the living room, Vera sewed and Jennifer did her homework. He read his book, necessarily, it seemed, and though all was in its place, when he glanced up at them from time to time, he could not help feeling an odd sadness.

The months passed and a year went by and then another. Jennifer drew away from the dependency upon him, and this seemed proper, but there were arguments. He hated arguments, yet he felt an obligation to say something whenever he smelled strange odors in her room, and he reprimanded her when her grades fell. He restricted her time on the weekends and generally did the things all parents do that are clumsy and ineffective. It was the last stronghold of his sense of obligation, and as she wore him down, he relinquished his authority over her to Vera.

And Vera amazed him. The image he had fashioned of her eroded as the months went by. She stopped eating the chocolate creams and joined a diet clinic. She exercised, smiling and puffing up at him from the living room floor, and her makeup took on subtle shades of purple and mauve. At first he thought that this was all to please him, offerings of gratitude and devotion. But then he realized the changes were for herself, for Vera. She who had thought herself undesirable now believed in desire, for she flirted with him sometimes and developed a nervous little laugh.

He came to dwell, finally, at the periphery of two females he had not expected to find, and the evenings he spent quietly in the living room seemed to lengthen. Cordiality and a sense of relief settled around them. It was foolish, after all, for people who had lived so long apart to struggle in a crazy world. And though he was shocked at times when he thought about what he had done, he came to relish the presence of others in the place where he lived.

And then one night, just after her sixteenth birthday, Jennifer went away with a dark-skinned man, and he never saw her again. He was left alone with a woman he hardly knew.

He now experienced the most peculiar sensations. For example, he could not control how he felt whenever Vera was gone for a few hours shopping or having her hair done. He paced about the rooms, looking at his watch or listening to see if he could hear her step in the hallway, and when she opened the door at last, he was always surprised and gratified.

He felt shy and embarrassed around her and had a hard time looking directly into her eyes, and yet his eyes followed her everywhere. He became solicitous. He moved from the far end of the dinner table and sat in Jennifer's chair so that he could fill her wine glass and hand her things. After dinner he would ask her what she wanted to do, and if she wanted to go out, he would ask where and take her there. He bought a twenty-four-inch color television and put it in the living room, and when she wanted to watch, he asked what channel and then sat next to her. He bought little gifts and gave them to her after work, lace handkerchiefs, black satin boxes of French perfume, and filigrees of gold for her neck. If she talked about a pair of shoes she had seen in a window or a purse or a dress, he asked which shop, and the following day a package arrived special delivery. He sat under the yellow lamplight only when she sewed or read a magazine, and he came to feel like a guest in his own house. All he wanted was to be near her, and in everything he gave her her way.

She became transformed. The exercise she had begun months before increased. She bought running shoes and shorts and every afternoon went flying through the park, past the lawns and steps and benches, where old men sat and watched her enormous breasts struggle upon her chest. She stopped eating meat and bought flour, cereal, and bread from a health food store around the corner. She consumed vitamins. Her waist grew slender. A man asked her to pose for photographs in the nude.

One day he stayed in his office during the noon hour to think, and Vera came in. She was wearing a bright blue dress with a uniform pattern of white marks all over it and bright blue shoes and a matching purse. The dress was pinched just above the hips and very flattering, and he thought she had come to see him and, with a peculiar sigh of relief, stepped through his door, but she only waved and stopped at Muriel Stratton's desk. Muriel took her own purse out of a drawer and they walked out together.

He closed the door to his office and sat down in the leather chair. He was perspiring. It was the first time Vera had come into the building since she had left it to marry him.

Thus began a series of engagements which she felt obligated to attend but which did not include him. One day in the street she ran into Todd Franklin, a salesman who had teased her mercilessly but whom she had liked anyway, and Franklin said, "Vera, is it you?"

"Of course it is, Mr. Franklin."

"Mr. Franklin?"

"Todd."

He asked her to have coffee.

Andrew Hampstead was like a man possessed. He wanted to know where she had been, what she had done. He wanted to know why she had gone. But he asked her nothing. Instead he wondered about her during the day and waited up for her to come home in the evening. She was kind. She always remained kind, no matter how beautiful she became, and she still managed to prepare his dinner most of the time and sit often with him in the living room or let him take her to the theater or to the museum. But it was never enough. Her independence grew and along with it his anxiety, which was only quieted when he was next to her. He could no longer read without her or sleep without her. He could not go to the mailbox without dreading what he would find or walk down the street without being frightened about what he might see. He had a hundred questions, a thousand questions, that were all one question too terrible to ask, so he only waited for her to call, waited for her to arrive, waited for her to return, in a solitude the likes of which he had never imagined, not even in his darkest hours, and then one night he waited all the way through into the morning, and what came back was a letter that said goodbye.

He was at the office when Muriel got to work. He held her wrist very tightly and discovered that Vera was on a plane to England. He rushed home, threw some things into a bag and caught the first flight for London.

He had learned where they were staying and took a room a short distance away in Victoria Station. He was outside their hotel waiting the following morning.

He followed them to Buckingham Palace and through St. James's Park. He followed them to Piccadilly Circus and then St. Paul's. In the afternoon he ate a steak-and-kidney pie, waiting for them to come out of Harrod's, and that evening waited in the dusk at Westminster Pier while they rode a boat up the Thames. The next morning they took the train to Dover and made the channel crossing to Calais. He followed them into Paris.

They were there two days, and he rode behind them in a cab while they took a tour bus to the top of Montmartre and back. He rode the underground to the Left Bank and loitered in the courtyard outside Notre Dame while they wandered about inside. He followed them in the morning to Austerlitz Station and bought a ticket behind them for the nine-thirty express to Barcelona.

He was as though hypnotized, creeping closer and closer to her on a mission he did not understand. It mattered less and less that she not see him, and once, while the train hurtled through the darkness, he peered into their compartment and found her resting against the window, her eyes closed. They arrived in Barcelona just before midnight.

The following day he felt drugged. He had not slept well any night of the journey, and the stubble of his beard was irritated by his shirt collar. He stumbled at some distance behind them as they strolled about town, but by late morning, when they went into the zoo, he was only a hundred paces back.

The zoo was like none he had ever experienced, with walkways above the animal pens and clear water running over bright stones. The animals were all animals he had seen before but with Spanish words on wooden posts to identify them, and it felt very strange to look at giraffe and water buffalo and not be able to pronounce the names.

It was there, standing before a group of ostriches, that she turned and saw him. She put her hand to her mouth and her face went white, but he waited on the gravel path and expected her to come to him.

Instead they hurried out into the dirty street, and he ran after them. When he caught them at the curb, waving frantically for a cab, Vera stared at him in abject fear, and he stopped short, confused.

"Vera," he called helplessly.

But they bounded into a cab and drove off. He followed.

They moved through the winding streets and arrived at a place that looked like a football stadium. People were milling about. He got out of the cab and saw Vera's golden curls bobbing through a sea of black hair. He pushed his way forward, watching her startled, frightened eyes turn back to him, and then he seized her by the arm.

"Vera," he pleaded.

He only wanted to ask, in all of this, from the very beginning, did she know that he did not love her? Was that why she had run away? But before he could speak, she screamed, and the man with her, a man he had never seen before, reached out and struck him in the face. He fell to the dusty pavement, and when he was able to raise his head, they were gone.

There was blood on his shirt. He sat for a moment wiping his nose. Then he stood up. People circled around him and into the stadium. He saw posters. It was a bullfight. He had read about bullfights once in a magazine, sitting alone beneath the yellow lamplight in his living room. They had seemed bizarre and unreal. Was Vera attracted to such things? He bought a ticket and went in.

There were benches arranged in concentric circles and down below, a ring of bleached sand. He sat down and looked about. Everyone had the same color hair and skin beneath the single, bright sun, and it should have been easy to spot her, but he couldn't see Vera anywhere. Perhaps they had come in and ducked out another entrance. He didn't know what to do.

Then there was the sound of trumpets, and men in flat little hats and brocade costumes in silver and gold stepped across the ring, followed by other men and horses. The men paraded, bowed, and left. Someone opened a door in the side of the arena and a magnificent black creature with white, tapered horns ran into the ring, pawed the sand, glanced wildly about and then stood, quite still, its nostrils flaring. A thin, dark man dressed completely in gold except for black slippers stepped out from behind a barricade holding a red cloth.

The dark man and the bull proceeded to dance, it was the only way to describe what happened then. Afterward a man on a blanketed horse pushed the point of a long lance into the shoulder of the bull and then other men ran around the head of the bull and stuck tiny, beribboned sticks into the same place. The bull and the dark man danced again, only the dance was smaller, tighter, it could have happened on the floor of Andrew Hampstead's living room, and then the man took the sword from behind the cape, held the cape in front of the bull, lifted himself to his toes and drove the sword over the head of the bull into its back. The bull wobbled, snorted blood, went down on its forelegs and rolled over, everything precise and exact and without chance.

As he watched, other strangely sad men, waving little red cloths, danced about the horns of the most dignified animals he had ever seen. One by one the bulls fell. The men strutted about the ring and were applauded.

And then, quite to his amazement, after everything had proceeded once again exactly through the first dance, the business with the lance and the beribboned sticks, then the second dance, almost to the point of boredom, the man with the red cape came forward with the sword above the glistening horns of a huge, black bull and was suddenly lifted into the air. The cape went flying, the man hovered for an ugly, long moment and then dropped like a bag to the sand.

There was a great noise from the crowd as others directed the bull aside. The man stood, bleeding from the thigh, and took the cloth in his hand. He hobbled to the bull, raised the sword, tried to drive it forward over the horns, and it popped away. Several times the man did this until finally the sword went in, and the man stepped back, waiting. The bull stood for a long time, its head lowered and swaying from side to side, and the man took another sword with a funny shape on the end and jabbed the bull behind the head, but nothing happened. Several times he did this, and the bull looked at him, blood streaming from its nose. The man jabbed and jabbed, and the crowd jeered, yet the man persisted in this foolish thing, all the while bleeding himself and getting weak. Then the bull went to its knees. The man took a dagger and tried again and again just behind the head. The crowd was truly jeering now, and someone came from the stands, grabbed the knife and with one thrust sent the bull flat to the ground. The crowd booed.

Suddenly the sky above the ring was very bright, and the faces of all the people were a gloom poised above the earth, and Andrew Hampstead began to laugh. In all the world no man was so ridiculous as he, in all the world no man, so absurd, but it did not matter. With happiness and delight, surrounded by scores of people who stared in disbelief at this stranger from another land, Andrew Hampstead laughed so hard that tears came to his eyes.

The dark man in the ring below looked up in amazement, smiled, and raised one bloody arm in salute.

Ace

The rains have come again. Another winter is upon me.

I stand at the window and look out. Beneath the great, gray sky the sheaf of water is interrupted by towering pines beyond my lawn. The needles of the pines make the water gather into silver darts that fall straight down into black puddles below. When I planted the trees thirty years ago, they were a foot high, and I had hair.

It is the first deep rain of the season, and Janice is not home.

My only companion, then, is Ace Bigelow, a mongrel cat I acquired at the SPCA several years before. Ace was of indeterminate age and parentage when I found him, having survived a vigorous burning episode with his previous owner, a despicable little Oriental man who was deported because of drugs. The Oriental, who had been known simply as I-Got, because he always delivered, flamed Ace in a desperate act of retaliation for losing the freedom this country so richly provides. Ace, the woman at the SPCA told me, was certainly more attractive before this event than he now appeared, one ear hairless and permanently flopped and a tail that had seen longer days. I only had to use my imagination, she encouraged. There were signs, as cats go, that Ace had once been quite beautiful.

So I named him for the most tragic companion of my childhood.

Janice, of course, cannot abide Ace. She endures him, as I do the wisps of curling paper that appear in her hair the evenings before we go to the Fergusons, the Houghs, the Woodalls, the Dederers; attend neatly carpeted dinners at Le Bistro, Grand China, Albert's, or any of the other teak-trimmed restaurants that have arisen to meet the tide of expatriates from San Francisco and Marin; sit in immaculate and perfumed silence where music is played, not spectacularly, or where bankers, sales clerks and insurance reps posture through Ionesco, Beckett, Oscar Hammerstein, Gilbert and Sullivan, much to the joy of the local drama critic.

After three marriages, one must compromise.

Ace is lying on the wallseat, his good ear raised against the rain, his once-grand tail like a hairy little club he keeps always at his side. His eyes are closed. His thick belly soughs evenly, like the gentle wind lifting the pine branches outside. Water comes off the edge of my roof in a steady current, crushing the jasmine below.

Homer Bigelow, by my reckoning, has been dead forty-two years.

Ace dreams, has nightmares, I believe, from that time with I-Got, when his life was secure, yet in jeopardy. He's dreaming now. The fur along his neck trembles. His whiskers jerk and pulse. A tic of nervous alarm rushes down his spine and cocks the stub of his tail. I have come upon Ace outside beneath a bush or shrub dreaming. I have seen rose petals shake and tiny, serrated creatures flee from Ace's dreams. I wonder, does Ace believe he is truly safe here, now, with me?

I first met Homer Bigelow the opening day of my second year at Lincoln Elementary, when, like something thrown out in the trash, he fell into the desk before me, a bundle of cotton scrap, bone, and filthy hair, which hung well below his pointed ears. He could not sit still, not even when Mrs. Larkspur, a graying, thick-ankled bison in a flowered dress, stood over him, arms crossed and face turned long-ingly to the west windows, beyond which September still bloomed with summer's memory.

"Homer," she said. "Homer Bigelow."

Homer glared, with a face made more fierce by the halfhearted attempt that had been made to wipe it clean. The other students, most of whom had passed with me through Mrs. Marbleton's kindergarten and Miss Hardin's first grade, and with whom I had established an easy alliance, turned to look. Homer reddened beneath the scrutiny, and I guessed, even then, that he was marked beyond redemption.

"Sit still," the bison said, wagging her finger. "You're a distraction."

No one knew what the word meant, but we understood that people like Mrs. Larkspur had a reservoir of such terms, into which they periodically dipped, to establish a superiority we could never overcome.

That afternoon, at recess, Homer had his first fight, bloodying Billy Nesbitt's nose and loosening a lower tooth which, the year before, Billy had pointed out to me with pride, because it had arrived late, cupped in behind the others. Homer was hustled to the principal's office, where he stayed through penmanship and a story about the letter "Z." We watched out the windows as a woman in boots, jeans, and a faded sweatshirt hurried across the west lawn to the school front door. I concluded that Mrs. Bigelow was one of the prettiest women I had ever seen, much prettier than my own mother, who was named, unfortunately, Esther. The next morning, when Homer returned, he was clipped, scrubbed, and quiet, though no one of us dared to think of him in any way but what we had observed of him that first day. The cause of the fight had traveled like wildfire. Billy had teased him about his name, a mistake forever ameliorated by Homer's scruffy fists.

I found out much later, when we had become friends, that his mother had named him Homer because, in school, she had studied the classics and because Homer's father, an itinerant dreamer, had wandered off three weeks after he was born.

So Billy Nesbitt's tooth was removed, Mrs. Larkspur stayed behind her desk, and the boy who sat before me, a scar on the nape of his neck as white as popcorn, was forever called, respectfully, Ace.

He bestowed friendship. It was not something earned, as with the older boys, certainly not the concrescence that gathers indiscriminately in childhood, like mud under fingernails. You were chosen, for reasons neither of you understood, since it was never discussed. But my father had been, to say the least, dictatorial, and had, one winter's night when I was three, died of a heart attack alone in the garage of our home, which left me distant and vulnerable, but alert. Perhaps Ace saw in me the echo of abandonment, as though our ships had been pulled together upon the beach and burned. Each day I examined that white, ragged scar, and when he turned to me, as he often did, for paper or pen, Ace must have seen in my eyes a wound of similar proportion.

Sometimes, even in childhood, there is a light of recognition, a knowledge of who we are, until the day we die.

I was a good student, a dutiful student. I read hard, plastic books with bright covers and wrote themes, my scrawl staying carefully between the wide, blue lines of my binder paper. I used a ruler to carve out the separations for my math problems. I practiced penmanship until my sentences began to look like those of Sally Hendrickson, who sat across the aisle. I studied geography, coloring, carefully, the shape of each mimeographed country. I spelled every new word again and again. I was hall monitor and traffic boy. I scissored and pasted. I was in the Thanksgiving Pageant, Christmas Play, and Spring Jubilee, never understanding, until much later, just what it was I was achieving, that the years of success at school were fashioning an inevitability reflected, even now, in the pale rain falling beyond my windows.

Ace didn't give a damn. His reports on the plastic-covered books were laconic and incomplete. He scribbled his math problems, hunting shortcuts to the equals sign. His penmanship was atrocious, but he could read the sentences, and that was all that mattered. He made blotches on the mimeographed countries, smears on the cut-outs and chalked misspelled words upon the blackboard until his fingers were bleached. Not in any pageant, play, or jubilee, he was, nevertheless, always down front, smiling up at me and winking one bright, blue eye. He winked at the blackboard, winked at his seat, turning to me for supplies, winked at recess, where he ran, jumped, and threw faster, higher and farther than anyone else. He did only just enough to get through and pass on. There was something he was waiting for, something that made all of this extraneous and unnecessary. He smuggled it into school in his lunch box, hid it behind his binder as he hurried through the tiresome work, strange, cardboard-spined books with no pictures and so many words my mind danced, books about places distant and unimagined, where something occurred, Ace declared, that was more real, even, than the chairs upon which we sat.

Because Ace knew, he let me know, since he had recognized how our ships had been destroyed, that he was smart, smarter than us all, smarter, even, than Mrs. Larkspur or any of the other teachers, whom, by necessity, only because he was yet small and burdensome, he allowed to occupy his time. While we scribbled or added, thinking we were learning, in miniature, what we needed to know later, he understood that we were all as horribly misaligned as the margins of our ruled paper, that what he longed for could never be discovered in straight rows.

Ace has stopped dreaming and seems content. The rain, perhaps, has filled the hollows where his demons live, and he floats, for a time, upon the veil of sound, like a ragged bird in flight. Often I have lain in a darkened room, gentled to sleep by the patter of tiny stones upon my roof. The reality of a world far beyond me, incomprehensible, unattainable, is transmuted by rain. Everything is small and quite manageable, and I am not afraid to be alone.

I went to Ace's house. He came to mine. Our home was a two-story colonial on Bedford Avenue. We had a large backyard, a swimming pool, a slide and merry-go-round, at the center of which Ace loved to lie, while the steel circle spun his head inches above the ground. Even though he had died young, my father, who was an investment broker, had accumulated a good sum of money, which he and my mother had wanted to spend on a large family. They had planned a beautiful life he had been forced to leave. No one else moved in. I was left with ghosts.

Ace lived in a two-bedroom flattop on Twenty-fourth, a block from the shopping center. His mother worked at the Social Services office during the day and sometimes other places at night. His room was bright, though, with pictures of mountains and rivers upon the walls. Twice a week his mother put fresh flowers on his dresser. He had a double bed, as did I. More than anything else, I enjoyed staying the night beneath Ace's walls.

His mother's name was Alison, but Ace called her Al. Sometimes, when my mother's friends were over, I heard them say Est to her, rather than Esther. I thought it sweet and close and, after hearing Ace say, "Al, Harry and I are going out," I wanted to call my mother Est, to see if I could find the peculiar trust and intimacy which Ace shared with his mother. In all the time I knew him, even from those first days, there seemed in Ace a life that had already been lived, that he and the woman who had given him birth, only a few years before, were much the same.

From the first, I knew my life with Ace would be an adventure, though, in his treatment of me, he was as predictable as the sunrise. The books he smuggled into class were maps. While I was content to be sure that the borders of my countries were properly filled, Ace laid plans to rebuild his ship so that he could set sail for distant lands. He told me about a place in Chile where the mountains were so high that the rivers which cut through them had never been explored. There were icy streams in Alaska where fishermen caught silver salmon as long as his arm, valleys in Australia where primitive people still carved life with flint and stone, hidden islands in the South Pacific where strange creatures mated and swarmed. When I used an orange crayon to fill in the outline of New Guinea, Ace described bizarre animals that hung from trees. When I wrote "Africa" upon the great continent, he drew a picture of a huge bull elephant, upon whose perfectly arched tusks a yellow lion was impaled.

Ace could draw.

He drew pictures of our teachers, pictures of the boys who challenged him after school and whom he always thrashed. He drew pictures of the things that had lived upon the earth long ago and imaginary beings who explored the universe in spaceships far more elaborate than any we saw in movies at the State Theatre. He drew a picture of Becky Witherspoon who, in the seventh grade, asked me to her birthday party—to which I could not go because I had pneumonia—that made me ache when Becky grew away from it.

In the fifth grade he drew a picture of his mother, naked, with her legs apart. He had come into the bathroom inadvertently one morning after she had taken a shower, and she had turned to face him, damp hair down about her shoulders, her body shining. The effect of this picture upon me was so intense that, from that moment, whenever I sat at Ace's dinner table, when we waited for her to fix sandwiches for our excursions into the country, when we watched her move about the house on those winter days when we played inside, I was closer to Al Bigelow than my own mother. The picture excited in me something I have never felt for any woman. One afternoon, the rain streaming outside, while we talked vaguely about life as something we would inherit far into the future, Ace held up the picture and said, "I could draw. I could go to all those places and just draw."

My heart beating, I studied the picture again, soft and suggestive in the gray light, and grew frightened. I did not want Ace to do anything more that would affect me like this.

And then, one Christmas, we were given bicycles, masts raised before the wind of boyhood. Ace was not content to ride in town. He wanted to pedal five miles out into the country, where fields were populated by pheasant and dove, where coyotes wailed, ducks flew, and snakes bellied beneath the grass. My mother never knew about these excursions. Common sense was a bond all mothers shared, she believed, and while she thought we only rode about the streets around Ace's house or the park nearby, Ace's mother packed a lunch and sent us off to reconnoiter the earth.

I was apprehensive much of the time, for Ace had no fear. He held my hand against a railroad tie just as the Southern Pacific freight tore past for Bakersfield. I heard the clamor and the roar and smelled hot steel and oil for hours. We went to Orange's Airport and ran out to touch the propellers of airplanes, until a watchman drove us off, shaking his fist. We went swimming nude in irrigation ditches, pretending that hideous serpents lurked behind the reeds and rushes. We found deserted houses and said they were castles or crawled far out into fields of corn until we were unutterably lost below the eight-foot stalks. One time an old man shot at us across grape vines. Another time a dog tore the leg of Ace's pants. And, most terrifying of all, I stepped once upon a rattlesnake, and it struck, thudding against my calf, a large rat clamped between its glistening jaws. Ace and I jumped back and stood, frozen, as the snake tossed the rat and coiled, ready to strike again. Ace made me sit down, and we watched the snake. I couldn't move anyway, but Ace smiled. "I wish I had a pencil and a piece of paper," he said. "His mouth was full, else he would have gotten you." We heard a noise and turned. When we looked again, the snake was gone.

Until the age of eleven, then, I thought of my life as, basically, Adventures with Ace. In the general fear and awe of growing up without a father, I was glad to move within the shadow he cast across my boyhood. His lack of interest in school opened my parochialism. His physical prowess and skill pushed me beyond mediocrity. And his ability to imagine himself in illusionary worlds, so poignantly expressed by the images he drew with casual but studied nonchalance, stimulated my mind and encouraged my heart. He never understood the effect he had upon me.

But someplace in the seventh grade, probably with my invitation from Becky, a turning point was reached, for I sensed, with the intuition only children can experience, that, inevitably, Ace and I would part.

I was awakened to this dramatically one afternoon when I came into the kitchen of Ace's house and found his mother seated at the table crying.

"Mrs. Bigelow," I said, wanting to touch her with a small, trembling hand.

"Never mind," she said, looking away and wiping her face.

"Why are you crying?" I asked. "Is something wrong?"

"It's nothing," she said, turning back. "Never mind."

I stood a long, awkward moment. The sense was blurred that I was just a little boy.

I thought of my mother, who had never remarried, dating sporadically between periods of long loneliness, and realized that, in all the years I had come there, I had not seen Ace's mother with a man.

I experienced a terror, at that moment, that I had never known. The sunlight came through the kitchen window and rested upon her hair. It was beautiful hair. I wanted to be older, old enough to take her hand in mine, to reassure, to tell her that I understood, I truly did, and that I would see to it that she would never be alone.

I stepped back, staring at her, embarrassed by a rush of desire I could not comprehend. Mrs. Bigelow looked at me and smiled, showing just the tips of two perfect, white teeth.

"You're a good boy, Harry," she said.

From that moment forward I wanted to be with girls.

Not Ace. He regarded creatures like Becky Witherspoon with a certain disdain, though sometimes, at recess, I caught him staring with narrow-eyed diffidence at Cathy Brownfield, who had just moved here from Wisconsin and was confused. I did not see it at the time— how could I?—but Ace, whose ship was being built for distant seas, understood that, at just this time, it was better to sketch them from afar, with simple detail, than to bring them close, for intimate scrutiny.

He knew, through the unconscious way, in childhood, that such things are known, just what they represented. While I tried them out, one after another, starting with Becky and then Elizabeth Wheeler, Melissa Scott, and Sandra Jepson, working my way into adolescence like a coal miner in a tunnel, Ace held them only occasionally at school dances, touched them momentarily at Saturday night parties, allowed them to sit beside him for brief intervals at the State Theatre. But there was no commitment, no intention, no need. He watched me soften beneath them and said nothing. His drawings of rugged hills and faraway, troubled lands became exotic to me. It was time to grow up. We drifted apart.

The rain outside has taken on a persistent uniformity that says it will last. It is cold in the house, and I should turn up the heat, but I do not want to feel an artificial warmth or to have the sound of the heater blow the tiny stones away. Rain makes me think, and right now I want to think. I button my sweater and put my hands into my pockets.

Ace Bigelow is curled into a furry ball, his nose unable to reach the stub of his tail. Free of ambition or the need to understand, he wears the scars of his suffering and is content to be. I want to pick him up and cradle him in my arms, but he does not enjoy being held. Though there is comfort for me in the roots of his hair, he is happy to preen himself and tolerate an occasional rub, because I have saved him. I named him well.

In high school Ace got into trouble. The increased regimen irked him, and he was often absent from class, but his mind, which had read and imagined so many things, pulled him along. He failed nothing. Neither, however, did he excel. I worried that one day, if he weren't careful, life would strand him, and he would end up on the beach with no way to go. Not even when he was suspended for fighting or made to feel guilty by the teachers we shared, who harangued him about his ability, which, they charged, he squandered shamelessly, did he change. "Education is water in the desert," Mr. Ames, our American history teacher, preached. "Without it, you will perish alone on the burning sand."

Ace laughed silently at me and winked.

When we got into our senior year and I was concluding, quite successfully, those things necessary to continue forward, I asked Ace one day, "But don't you want to go to college?"

He looked at me with those wide, clever eyes and said, "I don't know. Are you?"

"Of course," I said. "Have to."

"Why?" he asked.

"To be something. What else? Don't you want to study to be something?"

He shrugged.

"What do you want to be?" he asked.

"I don't know, for sure," I said.

He smiled.

"Besides," he said, "I don't have the grades."

"You could take the tests," I said. "They'd have to let you in. You know it."

He smiled again and winked. "It's an idea," he replied.

Halfway through that final year, when he turned eighteen, Ace dropped out of school and joined the army.

I never saw him again.

The Korean thing came on. I was at Berkeley for my degree in business administration and doing well enough to be deferred. Besides, I was the only child of a woman who had never remarried. There was a special status in that, and I was glad. Several times I received letters from Ace. He never said what was happening, but I knew it was bad. He included some drawings I could barely stand to see. In the last letter he wrote simply, "I know now what I'm going to be."

I came home one Saturday much later, when I was almost done, and saw Mrs. Bigelow going into a drugstore. I followed to ask about Ace. She told me he had been killed in combat the week before. I stood with her and we talked. The antiseptic, sweet smell of the room made me dizzy. "He did something," she said, "quite heroic."

There was an article in the paper one day. My mother saved it for me. He had been awarded the Medal of Honor.

So all the study, the filling in of all those lines had prepared me enough to survive, and I am more wealthy now than my father could ever have imagined. I have lived to marry and marry and marry again, to plant my trees and measure their growth thirty years into the nursery of old age, where I am clean and proper and cared for. And I never knew why he was called Ace.

The Monster

The trial of Mr. Arnold M. Spingler began on August 14, the hottest day of summer. Mr. Spingler came into the courtroom wearing a tweed jacket, woolen tie, and a pair of heavy gabardine slacks that accordioned over his thick, wing tip shoes. In the afternoon the air-conditioning failed, but Mr. Spingler did not loosen his tie or remove his jacket. His lawyer, in shirtsleeves, sweated profusely, but never a drop appeared on Mr. Spingler's brow, even when the prosecuting attorney, pointing a manicured finger, called him a monster without remorse and demanded that the jury condemn him to death.

Emile Pronocki, seated at the back of the room, never took his eyes off Mr. Spingler's neck, not even when the prosecutor began talking about the women.

The first was a Norma Friedel, an accountant for the Waygum Nursery over on West Montgomery. "A kind, generous woman," the prosecutor said, "with two grandchildren and a husband named Miller, who gave his life in the Vietnam War and was awarded the Purple Heart posthumously."

Mrs. Friedel was a woman of regular habits. She attended church each Sunday, sang in the choir, and did volunteer work at the hospital.

A concerned citizen, she rode on the bus with other protestors to dem-
onstrate against the Gardner Lumber Company that wanted to cut
down old grove trees near Deer Creek. She went to city council meetings to plead for the homeless when the shelter at the corner of
Twenty-fourth Avenue and Seymour was being debated and the
mayor's life was threatened. She sewed things for her grandchildren,
little Becky and Norman, who delighted in visiting her tiny, unpretentious home in the old section of town south of Harding Way.
And, finally, because there simply would not be enough time to detail every particle of this generous woman's nature, she baked apple
turnovers and icebox cookies for the meetings of Persons without
Partners, held the second and fourth Friday of each month at the
McKinley Community Center.

"I say finally, Ladies and Gentlemen of the jury," the prosecutor, a
middle-aged man named Spanini, said, "because it was her kindness
and generosity in this one of many endeavors which at last brought
her into contact with the man who would ultimately prey upon that
openheartedness, gain her trust, and then murder her viciously—"
(here he chopped the air with his right hand, making the diamond
on his little finger sparkle) "one night in his own home while the
neighbors slept."

Mr. Pronocki, who had not taken his eyes from the neck of Mr.
Spingler, blinked then and rolled up the sleeves of his cotton shirt.
The sweat poured from the prosecutor.

"Wanda Bieth was a kindergarten teacher, retired," he continued,
patting himself with an embroidered handkerchief, "who never married, yet had hundreds of adoring children, who spent an entire life
caring for the boys and girls of others. I dare say there are some,
seated in this very courtroom, who were charges of this kindly, self-
effacing woman, grown up now themselves, responsible citizens who
learned the first lessons of courtesy, respect, and love beneath her patient hand. A dedicated life that gave and never took. One of devotion and duty. A model of public service who, without a classroom at
last, without the very children to whom she had given all those years,
found herself, sadly, lost, alone, and, yes, even frightened. In other
words, Ladies and Gentlemen, vulnerable to someone without scru-

ples, a victim to someone without conscience, a trusting, unknowing sacrifice to—" (and here his finger went out again) "the evil monster who awaits judgment before you at this tribunal of justice."

Mr. Pronocki tried to understand the language of the prosecuting attorney. A man of little education himself, like Mr. Spingler, he found it difficult to concentrate on the neck of his old friend and at the same time string all the words together coherently. That Spingler was guilty, however, Mr. Pronocki hadn't a doubt. And it did not matter that, over the years, his friend had shown no attribute of character, no slip of the tongue, no silence or look that revealed the slightest inclination toward such atrocity. When the prosecutor raised his hand to chop the air over the memory of Emily Shaun, Eileen Rittenhouse, and Fran Nunnaly, Mr. Pronocki believed completely that his friend, Arnold M. Spingler, had established relationships with these unfortunate women, lured them to his home, hacked them to pieces with an ax, and then buried them without shame beneath the roses in his backyard.

In the afternoon the defense said that Mr. Spingler was insane, and the judge adjourned the court for the day.

Outside, Mr. Pronocki lit a cigarette and looked up past the buildings to the sky. He had been struck by how the two uniformed men had come to either side of Mr. Spingler but not touched him and how Mr. Spingler had walked from the room, not once looking at anyone, his shoulders squared, his chin lifted, like someone in a black-and-white movie who had been wrongly convicted. There was not a drop of moisture on Mr. Spingler's face.

Mr. Pronocki thought about going to the docks for a walk, as was his custom (he had been a longshoreman), but decided to go home instead. He went around to the screen door and entered through the kitchen. Emma was over the stove. Steam came up from one of the old aluminum pots. She was cutting potatoes.

"So," she said.

"They finished it for now," Mr. Pronocki replied.

"How much more?" she asked. He shrugged, and, though her back was to him, she answered, "You're crazy."

Mr. Pronocki went to the refrigerator to get one of the beers he had purchased at the Save-Mart the day before. It had been the habit of Mr. Spingler to accompany Mr. Pronocki to the Save-Mart on occasion, but only when Mr. Spingler needed to replenish staples that had been depleted over the previous month. Mr. Pronocki's weekly grocery lists, which his wife carefully prepared in four rectangles on three-by-five cards to match the departments in the store, were simply too much for Mr. Spingler's solitary needs, and so, by way of a joke, Mr. Pronocki sometimes bought a small bottle of rice wine vinegar, a two-ounce container of nutmeg, a package of bouillon cubes, something to make Mr. Spingler think his life was incomplete without a woman. The things stacked up in a cupboard of Mr. Spingler's kitchen, and one afternoon, when Mr. Spingler had stepped into the bathroom, Mr. Pronocki looked into the cupboard. Not one of the items had been used.

"Now that's filling," she said, bent over the pot. "You'll spoil the dinner." His hand around the cold bottle, Mr. Pronocki stared at the back of his wife's head. Her hair, which was very wiry, was bunched tight to the scalp like little springs. Her neck was thin and pale, made paler by the bright apron she wore.

Mr. Pronocki closed the refrigerator and went into the living room. The Kulwolski boy from up the street had not delivered the paper since Mr. Spingler had been arrested. His parents did not want him near Mr. Spingler's house. Instead he dropped the paper at the Rissbergers' on the other side of Mr. Pronocki, and Leonard Rissberger threw it over the hedge into Mr. Pronocki's front yard, where it invariably became lost down under the jasmine or the golden juniper. It didn't matter, however, because it was just more of the same, and on the television too. Arnold Spingler's blank, unsmiling face was everywhere.

Mr. Pronocki sat in the stuffed chair he had purchased thirty-two years before at Furniture Emporium and watched the afternoon sun touch the edge of the curtains. After awhile she called, and he went in to dinner.

They sat at opposite ends of the small table with all the food in the middle. It was boiled potatoes and beef again, which Mr. Pronocki liked, and he ate slowly, without looking up.

"Why did you go there, Emile?" she said at last. "I want to know."

Mr. Pronicki moved his water glass to the other side of the plate. He put his fork into a small peeled potato and twisted, so that the potato fell into two pieces.

"I haven't been able to sleep since the day they came for him," she went on, clacking the silverware. "Why?"

"He is my friend," Mr. Pronocki said.

"How can you be friends now with something like that? To think he came here day after day, over the years. He came for dinner. He came for breakfast." She held out her plate, which was almost empty, since she was a particularly fast eater. "Off these," she gestured. "These. I've scrubbed them all a dozen times. These spoons. It makes me want to throw everything away. To go down to March's Department and buy everything all over again. I can't bear to walk across the kitchen from the back door. Why couldn't he ever go around to the front like everyone else? You see, even there he was not normal."

Mr. Pronocki thought of the hole in the fence that separated his own yard from that of Mr. Spingler. Although he was meticulous about such things, Mr. Pronocki had never repaired the fence because it was simply easier to visit back and forth that way. He could not remember the last time he had gone through Mr. Spingler's front door.

Her jaw would be set now. The curls on her scalp would seem filled with electricity. The single vein between her flat, gray eyes would be filled with blood, twisted up her forehead to her hair like a piece of hard, blue string. He did not have to look to know what he had seen so many times.

Instead he watched the piece of dark, heavy beef situated just so upon his plate. Somehow it seemed proper that it might move, that, if he watched long enough and with complete attention, it might stand and walk away.

"Emile," she said.

"What?" he replied.

"I don't want you to go there again."

He did not say anything.

"It's not natural," she said. "I'm telling you now."

Even though he acquiesced in almost everything, there were times when, quite illogically, he must have his way. He did not say or do anything. He merely, on these rare occasions, had his way. She told him he reminded her of a petulant little boy who has been caught at something and has on his side only obstinacy. But sometimes she said nothing, if he were particularly quiet enough and steady. He stared straight at the piece of meat and stopped chewing.

After a time he heard her reaching and moving. He began to eat again. When he was finished, she went into the kitchen for the coffee and crumb cake.

He glanced at her when she handed him a piece and said, "What do you think makes people change now, Emma?"

Her face was sullen and drawn. When she was like that, she had, for a little, been defeated and would answer his questions directly.

"They don't," she said, stirring the lumps of sugar into her coffee. "Nobody changes. You are what you are, and that's all you are."

He stared at her, as though she had returned from a barren place, where, suffering alone for forty days and nights, she had discovered this one, immutable truth.

"But," he said, "Arnold."

"People are fools. Everything is there, but do they see it?"

"What does that mean?"

The look she gave him now was like none he had ever known, yet familiar, somehow, as his own shadow, cast down a dimly lit hall. The look spoke of years, rooms, furniture, money saved and lost, children grown up and gone away. It was over the top of things, like night on a desert, so that, when you came to the sunrise, full of hope and longing, what you found was not life, but nothing.

He turned away and felt the warmth beneath his collar.

"I'm going to throw these dishes into the garbage," she said. "All of them. I'm going to March's Department tomorrow morning. I'm telling you."

He could not look at her. It had been a long time that way. When he saw her face, it had to be when she was staring at something else, cooking or sewing or watching TV. For as many years as he chose to remember, they had slept in separate rooms. They had not gone dancing, which they once both had loved to do, since their last son Alfred's wedding eleven years before. Her mouth, that he had found so sweet that first night by the sea, now smelled of old linen stored away in a chest.

Did she know that musty loneliness? Had she comprehended, through these last, long years, more than an unwarranted bitterness and spite, which she wound closer and closer to her, like the coils upon her head? The thought that his suffering and pain were fastened upon her out of his own malice and ill will, after years of child-rearing and service, made Mr. Pronocki stop chewing and lay his fork upon the table. She was scraping at her plate with the edge of a knife, trying to remove some blemish or crust.

"Tomorrow morning," she said, looking up. "I'm telling you now."

Their eyes met, and something terrible turned inside Mr. Pronocki's heart. This leathery, mean woman was his. He, Emile Pronocki, had married her so long ago, yet she had become a stranger in his house. Youth was a dream beyond recall. The man next door, to whom he spoke through a hole in the wall, the way one prisoner might speak to another, had grown sweeter in his affection, as Emma Bueling, the girl he had once been so happy to find, was ground beneath the weight of resentment to this coarse, unleavened bread. He loved a monster more than his own wife.

Tears came to Mr. Pronocki's eyes. Something had been wrought upon him over the years which he was helpless to resist. Against the hope of the beginning, a force had come, as implacable, as uncaring as age itself. It built him a box, where children were born and emerged; where work, like the ticks of his watch, swung him between night and day, in comings and goings; and where the curls of Emma Bueling's hair, so soft in the darkness of that cottage by the sea, had turned to springs, twisting his heart to pain. This is what life had done. This is the way it used him, as it uses all living things. Unconcerned about Emile Pronocki, a rag upon a stick, it had returned him nightmares for dreams, despair for loneliness, a murderer of women for lost love.

He could not contain himself. He saw that she was right, that, whereas he had always felt cheated and abandoned, it was he himself, Emile Pronocki, who had become this thing. Wasn't freedom a door? Wasn't joy somewhere beyond the buildings? If he had given up, it was not a thing that someone else had done. It was what Emile Pronocki had done. Over the years life had not abandoned him. He had not moved with life. He was the fool. He went to the trial of Arnold Spingler, as he went through the hole in the fence which he refused to repair, to spite his wife. His fear and hopelessness were transfixed by the man next door.

He leapt to his feet, almost spilling the pitcher of coffee.

"Go to March's. Buy it all new. Everything. Buy whatever you want," he said, and ran from the room.

The following day he sat in the court watching the back of Mr. Spingler's neck. The defense attorney began an elaborate description of tenements and filth. Men came and went to an upstairs room, most of them drunken. They grunted, sweated, and swore, while a little one cowered behind a tattered sofa. When the little one cried sometimes between visits, the woman beat him. The men who saw him there or heard him whimper wanted to laugh, but most of them got up and went away, whereupon she beat him again. This was the woman who gave Mr. Spingler life. This was the childhood given to Mr. Arnold M. Spingler. A holocaust of emotion and pain, out of which had emerged this misshapen victim of incomprehensible neglect. From the promise of life, which is love, had been given torture and abuse. Any wonder, then, what path a boy might walk. Any surprise, then, what man might be found at the end of the journey. What mercy, given from those for whom the promise had been kept, might match such ugliness and pain. What compassion, even now, as these terrible crimes have been described, might triumph over such hate. To be without love is to be insane. To be insane is to be apart from the community of man. Such a fate is worse that the deepest hell. What good would it serve, then, to put him, who was already damned, to death?

No one moved. Only the air-conditioning, which had been repaired, blew a thin breath of sound into the room. The defense attorney had been as eloquent as the prosecutor. He stood, shaken and bent, staring at the jury, as though he himself were on trial. Mr. Pronocki saw Mr. Spingler's head go down. With that, he stood and left the court.

He did not attend any more of the proceedings, even though they extended, because of technicalities, into the following week. When Mr. Spingler was at last found guilty, Mr. Pronocki went to the prison.

They let him in because he was the only one who came. He was led into a tiny room without windows and divided by Plexiglas. In the middle of the room was a small shelf against the Plexiglas and a stool. He went to the stool, sat down, and leaned upon the shelf. A door opened. His old friend was escorted by a tall, uniformed man to a stool on the other side of the Plexiglas. Mr. Pronocki looked through the sheet of transparent material, where he saw both the face of Mr. Spingler and the reflection of his own.

He stared into Mr. Spingler's eyes, which were as simple, plain, and ordinary as before. Mr. Spingler stared too. They sat a long time. Mr. Pronocki could smell that something sweet had been sprayed into the room. Mr. Spingler wore a starched blue shirt that was one size too large. Then he opened his mouth, and Mr. Pronocki sat back.

"They say I am a monster," he said. "You have come to visit the monster, Emile."

"I had to come," Mr. Pronocki said.

"You will not be here again," said Mr. Spingler. "It is not necessary."

Mr. Pronocki could not speak. He only saw the one he had known for so many years. It was unthinkable that Mr. Spingler should be here, but he was.

"Ask, then," Mr. Spingler said. "You came here to ask something. Go ahead. Ask."

Mr. Pronocki shook his head.

"Then I have nothing to say," said Mr. Spingler and made a motion to leave.

Mr. Pronocki leaned forward, his hands on the transparent material. "Then I will," he said, wetting his lips. "Did you like my wife, Arnold?"

Mr. Spingler's eyebrows went up. "Who?" he said.

Mr. Pronocki stood and backed away. Mr. Spingler began to smile. "Who?" he said again, showing his teeth and growling a bit.

Mr. Pronocki bumped against the door. He fumbled for the knob. Mr. Spingler sat there, smiling.

He did not go home, even though it was late. He went to the docks. At night the river was oily and dark. It seemed larger than it was, joined to something darker and deeper. He stood at the foot of a pier looking down. He was so terrified by what came into his mind that he couldn't move.

He fell to his knees. What else was there to do? He longed for dispensation, and he knew that Emma Bueling was without appeal. The only hope lay beyond the stars, in something to which, for the longest time, he had not turned, something that, he believed even now, at the bottom of his lonely heart, was not there. In the darkness by the river, with all the ships tethered to the shore, Emile Pronocki prayed for his soul.

The Mouse

Carsten Ulrich knew a mouse when he saw one. Little eyes glowing in the lamplight. Soft, pale-smooth flesh. Pointed, nosy face. Dry, quick nails skittering from beneath drab sleeves, scratch-sliding over every surface.

She came into the office that afternoon and sat down quietly at the desk of old Pecchenino, who had died of lung cancer a week ago Monday. It had been an awful funeral. Carl had watched the floor the whole time. Someone had worn rose-scented perfume. He had shut his eyes and thought of spring, until the organist missed a note and started again. There were only a few people from the office. Pecchenino had bad breath and no friends.

The desk had been empty for nearly two weeks, which allowed him to keep the lights dim, except for those just above his station, so he didn't notice the door to the outer office open that Friday afternoon, nor hear the slippered pad of small feet hurrying to Pecchenino's desk. Though he understood that Mr. Whitmarsh could not long tolerate inactivity, he had come to enjoy the relief from the old man's coughing and the quiet shadows of each day, deepening gently toward the hour when he could go home.

His back was to the room, as he concentrated upon the numbers within the green window of the computer screen. The first thing he heard, then, was the scratching. She was moving things out of a cloth bag across Pecchenino's bare, wooden desk, holding the things in the tips of the fingers so that the nails skittered here and there, testing the dark. She didn't say a word. When the bag was empty, she stood and padded straight to the door. After she was gone, he went to the front of the desk, where she had carefully placed a polished brass plate. It had one word: Bellefeuille.

Ten minutes passed, and he hadn't touched the keyboard of his computer, when the door opened again, and she padded across the floor, carrying a cardboard box. He kept his back to her, hunched forward, pretending to work. More scratching. Then a pale glow fell upon his hands. She had set up a lamp. He couldn't very well refuse to notice then, so he turned, trying to find, in the remnants of his week, one last, wan smile.

All he saw was the eyes in the pale light, then her remarkable smallness. Her elbows just reached the top of the desk. Her toes were on the rungs of the chair, her shoes, plain leather flats, placed heel to heel on the floor. About her body was draped something that blended with the rug. She had plain brown hair cut straight above her ears and trimmed square just below her neck. Her face was narrow, her brows very thin. She blinked. The glow snapped off and on.

"Carsten Ulrich," he offered the stumble of his name.

"Bellefeuille," she replied, looking away, "Hermione Bellefeuille."

He turned, trying to recall where he had heard such a sound before. He thought he must watch her a bit more, but she began spreading manila folders in a neat semicircle about the desk. He turned to the computer, where nothing had happened, and waited for the day to end. At five-thirty precisely she rose from Pecchenino's chair and padded directly to the door. When, without turning, she shut it briskly behind her, he put his head down carefully upon his folded arms and closed his eyes.

He lived alone in a two-room flat above a delicatessen on West Montgomery. His best friend, that is, the one person he saw most often, was Harry Lagomarsino, who worked in the delicatessen during the week and gave him an extra spoonful of macaroni salad or slice of Gouda when he came in to find something for the evening meal. Harry called him Car. Nobody had ever called him Car, and he was offended at first, until he heard the owner, Mr. Offerman, one day yell, "Hare!" at the bald, fat man, who had just dropped a roll of salami to the floor. So one day he said, "Hare," when ordering a quarter-pound of liverwurst and a pint of coleslaw. Harry looked up, grinned, showing two gold teeth, and said, "Hey, Car, you want to maybe come over tonight and watch the fight, since the missus is at her sister's, who is sick?"

He put on a smile, shrugged a little.

Harry took this for approval and said, "So don't get anything, then. I got plenty. And beer too. Seven o'clock."

Harry lived two blocks away in a small walk-up that looked into an alley. There were knickknacks everywhere. Family pictures on the walls. Oval throw rugs that Harry's wife, Oma, had made from scraps of yarn she found at Miller's Department Store downtown. Paper-thin doilies on the arms of the chairs. He thought of his Aunt Danene's house in Montana, where he had gone once as a boy. In the living room, which was crammed with stuffed furniture and shining glass animals, the television was already on.

Two black men were fighting. Harry put him in a mohair chair before a folding tray, where he sat forward, eating the hot pastrami sandwich and drinking Heineken. The muscular figures beat each other mercilessly. He could barely swallow. The images blinked and flickered. The colors blurred. The sweat on the men made them look like enormous, jointed eels, twisting and lashing within a white, rectangular box. He could barely move. Harry threw his arms about, shouting and swearing, stamping his feet. The fighters became one shine of muscle and glove, interrupted every few minutes by automobiles spinning on platforms or bare women using exercise machines, where Harry tried to talk to him, bring him a beer or fill his plate, but where he only sat, chewing frantically before the next round began.

When the fight was done, Harry shut off the television, but

Carsten remained quite still, his heart pounding, expecting something more. Then Harry said it was over, and Carsten got up and went home.

Carsten did not have a television himself. He was terrified by the power of television. He had owned one once as a young man, when President Kennedy was assassinated. He had watched in horror all day, every day, everything about what happened, the long, slow drumroll of pain, the march of commentary, all the specials, and then, when they were done, anything fraught with emotion, no matter how tawdry, anything where people cried or struggled or died, any cheap serial or soap opera. He did this every spare moment from work, all day on Saturday and Sunday, and far into the night during the week, until, one evening, the tube blew and he was left in the dark, listening to the beating of his heart.

He did not repair the television. He kept it in his room, against the far wall by the window, looking from time to time at its blank, gray face as he read books.

He read Guizot's *History of France* and Mommsen's *History of Rome.* He read Prescott's *The Conquest of Mexico* and *The Conquest of Peru.* He read Plutarch's *Lives* and Schiller's *The Thirty Years' War.* He read Gibbon, Froude, Grote, and Beard. There was a certainty about the past. Images of great people, triumph and defeat, filled his mind, yet all was as still and finished as the objects that occupied the bins in the delicatessen below.

Sometimes he needed socks or underwear, but he did not dare walk through the appliance section of the department store where he shopped, even though that was the shortest way. There they had televisions, dozens of them, all showing the same thing. One day he had thoughtlessly found himself staring suddenly at a dozen of the same scantily clad young woman, tap-dancing across a wooden floor. The muscles of her legs made his throat hurt. He went to the boxes, twisting the knobs so that each set had a different picture, until the floor manager came over and told him to stop, that's how people made comparisons.

He bought a new set when Clarence Thomas and Anita Hill were on. He watched every moment of the hearings, and then the analyses and the specials with Peter Jennings and Dan Rather, the interviews and the replays. When that was done, he watched Oprah and Phil and Geraldo. He watched *As the World Turns* and *Days of Our Lives.* The television had a VCR, so he taped the shows he could not see while at work. He watched *General Hospital, Guiding Light, Wheel of Fortune.* He ate his dinner on a metal tray. He bought *TV Guide* and watched what was on Monday evening, Tuesday evening, Wednesday evening. He stayed up late Thursday evening, Friday evening, and Saturday evening. He could name the characters on *Murphy Brown* and *Northern Exposure.* He knew all the actors' names. One night, at ten-fifty, during a soap commercial and just before a rerun of *Highway Patrol* with Broderick Crawford, he lifted the set and dropped it out the window to the street below.

When he returned Monday morning, she was hunched over the old man's desk, scratching at the manila folders. He sat down quietly and removed the herringbone jacket he had bought at a President's Day sale the year before. Mr. Whitmarsh was concerned about the Breckenridge account, on which Pecchenino had been working, so there was a tremulousness to the silence he drew about him. His hands were damp when he pulled the dustcover from the computer.

He could just see his reflection and tried to make out the eyes, which were the same color as the screen. He opened his mouth. Something shone, far back in the glass, and winked out when his lips closed.

He opened his thermos and filled the aluminum cup. He liked his coffee very strong, much stronger than they made it at the machine out front. The hot, burnt smell pushed back the scent the office took on from being closed over the weekend and reminded him of a cafe one might see in a black-and-white movie, with people like Charles Boyer and Hedy Lamarr. When he replaced the cap, he heard the wheels of Pecchenino's chair and the sound of slippered feet. Then she was beside him, just above his shoulder, and a glass jar appeared, at the bottom of which were arranged thin, yellow wafers.

"That smells so nice," the voice said. "You might like one. I make them myself. They go well with good coffee. The jar is right on my desk. Bellefeuille. Hermione Bellefeuille. Just help yourself."

He picked a wafer from the jar and held it in his fingers. "Thank you," he said. "Thank you so much."

She returned to the desk and sat down. He watched her move her feet onto the rungs of the chair. Her fingers skittered about the folders. Her small head bobbed.

He put the wafer to his lips. It had virtually no flavor, but he picked up the aluminum cup and took a sip. When he bit into the wafer once more, he wanted to drink again, and the coffee tasted even better.

He rummaged through the bottom drawer of his desk and found a styrofoam cup. He brought it to her with the thermos.

"Would you, perhaps, care for some?" he asked.

"Why, yes," she said. "But I have a cup."

She produced a plain white porcelain mug and set it upon the desk. He poured the coffee and cleared his throat. She nodded, then took a sip.

"Yes," she said, moving the glass jar toward him. He took another wafer and returned to his desk.

"Ulrich," he said, as an afterthought. "Carsten Ulrich."

"Yes," she said. "From Friday."

They did not speak again the rest of that morning. When she got up once to leave the room, he stepped to the desk and refilled her cup. In the afternoon she asked him a question about the Breckenridge account. He said he didn't know, that it was strictly the work of old man Pecchenino, who had died of cancer. Then it was quiet until five-thirty, when she arranged the folders into a neat pile, went straight to the door, and closed it firmly behind her. He sat alone for twenty minutes before placing the dustcover carefully over the computer, turning out the light and going home.

The following morning he found a glass jar on his desk, at the bottom of which were arranged thin, yellow wafers. Stunned, he sat behind the computer and stared at the jar, which gleamed dully in the soft light. The day before, after work, he himself had gone to the All Night Drug to buy a thermos twice the size of the one he had used for twenty years. It was full beside him and made his hand sore a little, carrying it here from the apartment.

He rolled the chair forward and removed the lid. He put his nose into the jar and inhaled. There was a faint scent of anise, then something that reminded him of metal trays resting in the sun. It was a very pleasant smell, and he closed his eyes. In that moment the door opened quietly and she came padding to Pecchenino's desk, where the manila folders, without his notice, had already been spread out. When he heard the scratching sound, he clamped the lid down with such force that the reverberation startled him.

He did not say a word, but immediately removed the dustcover from the computer and worked frantically for half an hour before turning. There, on the near corner of the old man's desk, was the white porcelain mug. He unscrewed the cap from the thermos, rose slowly, traversed the short distance, and poured the coffee. The brown head bobbed once, twice. He returned to his desk.

He wanted to crawl into the computer, where, exact and precise, numbers and figures waited, knowing just what to be. Then there seemed an inordinate amount of scratching at Pecchenino's desk. Once she rose and came to his side, holding the empty mug. He filled it immediately and caught her staring at the glass jar. He nodded too, tried to smile. When she went back to her chair, he wanted to remove the lid, to take a wafer, but his hand shook. A short time before lunch, he heard the folders being moved. When he turned to look, she was striding to the door.

She did not return after the noon hour. He went to Pecchenino's desk and stared at the bronze nameplate. The folders made a perfect semicircle, like a miniature moat, before the old man's chair, on which she had placed a plain cushion.

Confused, he returned to his desk and removed the lid from the jar. He put his hand inside. The wafers were grainy. He had liked the feeling on his tongue. He picked one and put it into his mouth.

She did not come back, and, as the afternoon wore on, he devoured the wafers, drank the rest of the coffee and was still waiting, he knew not what for, when the evening shadows came on and the building grew quiet. That night he had a hard time sleeping, but when he returned to the office the next morning, there on his desk was the jar, full to the top with thin, yellow wafers.

He took all the room he needed now, circling the floor, sniffing the air, curious about what might come next. Not once did the jar grow empty, and he saw to it that the mug, which was placed always just so at the corner of the old desk, stayed full, until around eleven, when it disappeared into the cloth bag and he knew she was done.

In the heart of Carsten Ulrich there was no place, over the years, to which he had not withdrawn. As others might seek new lands, to find, in the journey, the mystery of themselves, he had narrowed all life's search to one small cubbyhole where, should the world grow haphazardly dark, he might yet find his way. Though lonely, he was justified in living alone, and those who came into his world did so at no risk, for he demanded nothing. From home to office, from office to home and the long, silent hours of reading, thought, and sleep, he fed upon himself and was satisfied that others were foolish and strange. Like passersby on a crowded street, they bumped against him and moved away.

Anything new, therefore, must be so unobtrusively, as dust gathering along a windowsill. No event could ever be so powerful as the accumulation of his life.

After a time, then, he took no specific pleasure in preparing the large thermos. Neither was it a chore he might otherwise avoid. The appearance of wafers each morning coincided with the serving of coffee, and it seemed that, whatever he had experienced at first, the two actions now struck a balance, canceling each other out.

He did not use her first name, nor did she use his.

"Would you ever like some different kind?" she once asked. "Ginger are good. Or perhaps cinnamon."

"No," he said, "these are fine. Would you care for some other blend sometime? They have all sorts."

"Oh, no," she said. "This is just fine too, just the way you have it now."

The coffee and wafers were utensils. He stopped thinking about them.

One day an odor appeared in the room. He wrinkled his nose, sniffing the air. It was a burnt, sweet odor. He turned to look at her. She was hunched over the folders, her feet on the rungs of the chair, her head bobbing. She was wearing the garment she had worn the first day.

It wasn't an unpleasant odor, just particular, something that reminded him of the back of a flower shop or the colored advertisements in some sales magazines. He stood carefully and pretended to go to the cabinets where the records were stored. He glanced at her and just caught her ducking down. Then he spotted it near the window by the copy machine, a round little tub with some sort of oriental design. A candle was burning in the tub, and above was another tub with the same design. The odor came from there.

"Oh, I hope you don't mind," he heard her say, "but it's so nice."

"What is it?" he asked.

"Potpourri. You pour in these scented flakes. The candle heats the water. The odor aspirates."

"Aspirates," he said, bending over the tubs.

"Yes," she said. "Releases. Like breath."

He circled to his chair and sat down.

"I'll remove it, if you like," she said. "But the days are getting warmer. Sometimes it's musty. Have you noticed?"

"Musty," he said.

"I'll put it out, then," she said. "It's not really important."

"No," he replied, oddly teased, "don't."

"They have different scents," she said.

"This one," he said, "is all right."

After awhile it only smelled like polished furniture. He stopped thinking about it.

One day she brought a new leather briefcase to the office. She stepped in, grasping the handle with both hands, leaning back against the weight. He went over and took it from her.

"Oh, thank you," she said. "Just by the chair, then, please. Thank you."

He did not ask about it. She volunteered nothing. At the end of the day, she placed an armload of folders into the briefcase, picked it up with a puffy exclamation and went straight out the door, leaving it open behind her. He walked over to close it, and there she was, leaning back like a bricklayer, struggling through the outer office toward the elevator.

The following day he went down to the street with her, holding the briefcase in one hand and the thermos in the other. He followed her to the subway entrance, which was in the middle of the next block, and watched as she moved down the steps, one at a time, the briefcase knocking at her legs.

Something was satisfied within him. Each day he met her at the office door, took the thick briefcase to old Pecchenino's chair, consumed dark coffee and yellow wafers until eleven, ate lunch alone at his desk in a room that smelled pleasantly of new furniture, and then, just after five-thirty, helped her carry the burden of her work to the subway steps, where, clumsily, she disappeared into a hole until the following morning.

He was reading Rawlinson now and Hallam. People were artifacts in a museum. He bent close, examined carefully, though he could not touch, nor did they speak or move. The images of them filled his mind near sleep, like photographs in his mother's albums. Hermione Bellefeuille was as much a part of the routine of his life, now, as Harry Lagomarsino, who called him Car. He stopped wondering about her.

So it was that she never actually invited him to dinner. Neither did he seek any of her time. One evening he simply found himself before an apartment door on West Thirty-fourth, the leather briefcase, heavier now, in one hand and the thermos in the other.

He sat at a small mahogany table covered with a plain brown cloth. She brought in several bowls of steamed vegetables and a basket of multigrain bread she had baked herself. He added salt to the vegetables, a pat of butter to the bread. The coffee she served tasted like his own. There was a dish of yellow wafers.

"Would you like to watch some television?" she asked, when they were done.

He looked carefully about. The walls were white. There were no pictures. The dining area was separated from the living room by a raised partition on which were placed clay pots of artificial flowers. In the living room were two stuffed chairs, a sofa, end lamps, a coffee table and, against one wall, a small desk. Near the window, which opened to the street below, was a thirty-two-inch television set.

She stood quickly, holding the pot of coffee in one hand and his cup in the other. She padded into the living room and set the things on the table, returned for the plate of wafers and smiled. Her small white teeth shone. Her eyes blinked off and on. He went into the room and sat in one of the chairs. She perched on the sofa. All the furniture faced the screen.

"Why don't you find something, then?" she said, nodding at the table and refilling his cup.

He picked up the *TV Guide*. Tiny black checks had been made in every time period.

They watched *Jeopardy* and *University Hospital*. They watched *Picket Fences*, then a film called *The Seventh Voyage of Sinbad* with Kerwin Mathews. He drank coffee, ate wafers. He hardly knew she was there, until a commercial about motorcycle lawyers came on. He realized it was eleven-thirty, and went home.

The next morning she arrived at work with a bandage wrapped around her wrist. He took the briefcase immediately and set it at the foot of Pecchenino's chair. She took out the porcelain mug and went over to light the candle between the oriental tubs. He poured the coffee and removed the dustcover from his computer.

That night she served something that had been baked in a pot of wild rice. There was a bowl of mixed vegetables, a basket of multi-grain bread. With the coffee she served a dish of cinnamon wafers.

"For something different," she said.

Two candles flickered in the center of the brown cloth.

He bit into a cinnamon wafer, wrinkled his nose. She told him she had never had any trouble finding work, she was very good, but that she had quit her last job and the one before because of the people.

"Why was that?" he wondered.

"I didn't like them," she said.

After dinner they went into the living room. She handed him the *TV Guide* and lit the fresh candle that rested between two tubs like the ones in the office.

He said, "I've worked for Whitmarsh & Sons for thirty-two years." She nodded and said, "I'll tell you when it's eleven-thirty."

They watched *Wheel of Fortune* and *Seinfeld*. They watched *Five Million Years to Earth*, with James Donald and Barbara Shelley. Then they watched *David Letterman* for a half hour, and he went home.

More often than not now he found himself after work seated at the mahogany table, waiting for what she brought in from the kitchen. In a very short while he came to recognize everything she prepared. The flavors took on a pattern into which he relaxed, as he did the stuffed chair in the living room. After a time the briefcase seemed no longer heavy, she stopped bringing it altogether, but he went there anyway, every night except Saturday and Sunday.

The weekends grew strange. He was reading Oliphant and Constant. Napoleon became a figure in a science fiction movie; Savonarola, a character in a Warner Brothers cartoon. He tried to read newspapers and magazines. He went through the shopping catalogs that arrived in the mail. One Saturday afternoon he found himself in the department store, undecided about what to do, trembling before a score of television sets, each with the same face.

The following Monday, after the coffee had been poured and the candle had been lit, she said, "Last night you missed *Orchestra Wives* with George Montgomery and Lynn Bari. Saturday night they had Sherlock Holmes in *The Hound of the Baskervilles* with Basil Rathbone and Nigel Bruce, right after *Biography*, which I know you like. Why don't you come over on Saturday and Sunday to watch? It's all the same to me."

So he was there seven nights in a row now, staying longer on Saturday and Sunday. The images on the thirty-two-inch screen began to blur. He was not sure if he had seen the movies before, and the half-hour shows ran together, like commercials.

On the weekend she dressed differently, in sleeveless, open-necked dresses that fell straight to the floor. She wore mascara and dark lipstick. She piled her hair atop her head. In the candlelight the flesh beneath her ears was as unused as the underside of something in a pet shop waiting to be purchased.

One Saturday night he fell asleep in the chair and awoke with a woolen blanket around him and the smell of fried bacon in the air.

"You looked so peaceful," she said. "I hadn't the heart."

He ate breakfast and went home. Sunday afternoon was disjointed and unreal, until he was at her apartment that evening, seated at the mahogany table and staring at the blank screen in the other room while she carried things in from the kitchen.

"It seems so silly," she said, standing up and stretching the following Friday night. "With all the good things on at the end of the week, I mean, and everything so late. Here, I bought you a present. They've already been washed. Good night."

She went into the bedroom and closed the door. He opened the bag. Inside were plain gray pajamas. The woolen blanket had been placed carefully on the floor near the chair.

He looked at the pajamas, then touched them with the tips of his fingers. They were flannel, just what he liked. He put the pajamas on the coffee table and sat down in the chair. He looked at the thirty-two-inch screen, where his reflection was still happening. He took the pajamas and held them up. They were gray flannel pajamas with a white drawstring.

It was a long time before he got everything off and the pajamas on. Then he sat down in the chair and pulled the blanket over him. He fell immediately to sleep and awoke in the morning to the smell of fried bacon.

This went on until it no longer mattered, anymore than the toilet things which accumulated for him in her bathroom, until one night she suggested that it must be so uncomfortable, the chair was so cramped and the sofa so short, why didn't he simply come into the next room with her and use the bed.

"It's kingsize," she said, "and like sleeping in a loft."

She picked up the blanket and went into the bedroom. He watched through the door as she sat on the edge of the bed at the far side, fluffed the pillow, let down her hair, and then crept beneath the blankets, where she disappeared. He watched longer, until the blankets rose and fell regularly.

He looked about the room. The walls were bare, the furniture drab and empty. In the kitchen the refrigerator hummed. There was a noise down in the street. The television was an enormous eye that had finally closed.

He removed everything and drew on the flannel pajamas. He arranged the clothes in a pile on the chair and stepped into the bedroom.

The room was bare too, except for the bed and one dresser against the far wall. There was the scent in the air of something burnt and sweet. He went to the empty side of the bed and stood quite still.

She made almost no impression, gathered as far away as possible. He saw only the back of her head, which looked for all the world like a tiny animal that had crawled onto the pillow.

He had not realized the hour had grown so late. He was very tired. Slowly he turned and allowed himself to stretch prone upon the bed.

"Turn out the light," she said softly.

And he did.

Never Trust the Weatherman

At last he was settled comfortably, it was still raining hard, the sidewalks were crowded, the other cabs were taken, when he saw the woman standing at the curb waving her arm frantically. He told the driver to pull over.

She did not see him, huddled there in the corner, so that when the door opened and she poked her head in, she pulled back abruptly, as though slapped.

"It's a miserable night," he said and smiled. "We can share, if you don't mind."

She nodded and came sliding onto the seat. The water poured from her jacket, making puddles and streams, one of which reached his thigh. He frowned, crossed his legs, but resolved to remain chivalrous. For the first time since the divorce, the judge had decided in his favor about money.

"Thank you," she said, in a voice as wet as her clothes.

He looked at the back of the cab driver's head, thinking, well, he had done the right thing. But the driver sat, hunched under his cap, content to watch the people scurrying across the street.

He tried to see her out of the edge of his eyes. "So," he said, "I suppose closest should go first. I live on West Montgomery."

"I do too," she said.

He turned.

"The twelve hundred block."

"The next," she said.

She took a round woven basket from beneath her jacket and set it gingerly upon her lap.

"It's too big a city," he replied, making his voice deep and even, "for so much coincidence."

He wished he hadn't said it. He hadn't even seen her face. But such things were as natural in his mouth as Macanudo cigars. He offered them in the anonymous places one finds women, elevators, hallways, theater lobbies, the boarding lines of air terminals.

"Perhaps," she said, without turning, "it's just irony."

He didn't understand and felt a bit miffed, after all, that he had given in to sentiment. He touched his damp leg and imagined her standing in the rain.

He gave the driver his address.

The cab moved slowly through traffic. Intermittently, it found pockets of downpour, when the lights outside became smeared, the windshield wipers barely carried away the water, and the sound of the heater was lost to the clamor upon the roof. Finally the rear windows became covered with a beaded film of gray, and he lost sight of where he was. He tried to straighten himself in the corner and noticed that she pulled the basket closer, resting one hand on either side.

He did not like sitting alone with a woman in a dark place and not talking. It made him think of uncomfortable things, like waiting with his shirt off in a doctor's office or running to miss a connection between flights. True or not, there seemed a personal judgment attached to such events, for which he was always ill-prepared.

The air in the cab was close. He opened his coat a bit and cleared his throat. She stared straight ahead.

"The weatherman says this is supposed to blow over tonight," he offered, "and tomorrow morning will be clear."

Tomorrow was Saturday and he was particularly looking forward to some time to himself.

She shifted a little but would not turn.

"If you can trust what he says," she replied, and leaned into the corner away from him.

He was content to let it go at that. He was so sensitive to women that he could almost know, watching them across a crowded room, exactly where they were coming from. If it had been hard enough, when they all looked like June Cleaver, the missionaries among them now made life impossibly complicated. They were easy to spot, though, even before they opened their mouths. You could see it in how they dressed, how they wore their hair, how they walked or held a knife and fork. The secret to any kind of tranquility was to avoid them like the plague. If there was one thing he had learned from two marriages, that was it.

It took twenty minutes to get through all the traffic to West Montgomery. By that time he had forgiven her even the tiny current against his thigh.

"What's your number?" he asked.

"My number?" she replied, facing him for the first time.

"Where you live," he said. "I'll drop you off there and drive back. It's still coming down pretty hard."

She fumbled for her purse.

"I'll pay my half."

He felt a bit triumphant and waved his hand. "Forget it," he said. "It's only a block. What's a block?"

"But I insist. Really."

"Never mind," he said. "*I* insist."

She was silent a moment, then said, "Just the corner, then. That will do."

"The corner? It's raining cats and dogs."

"Just the corner. Please."

When she got out under the street light, he was able to see her legs, which were quite shapely, and the wet shine of her face, which was well proportioned but plain. It was difficult to tell because she kept it lowered, clutching the basket to her chest.

"And thank you," she said.

The driver made a U-turn and headed back. He rubbed the glass, trying to see where she went, but she stood waiting until the cab was swallowed by the storm.

It was raining the next morning when he crossed the street to the Espresso Cafe to have breakfast. He did not come here as often as he might like because it was inhabited by a certain clack of women who wore nose studs, no makeup, and Mother Earth costumes that touched the floor. But the coffee was very good, and sometimes luck was on his side.

It was this morning, when he opened the door, smelled the ground beans, and saw Manny, the owner, wave at him.

The place was full, however. The rain was responsible, driving people from the solitude of dark rooms to the huddled companionship of maple syrup, Canadian bacon, and foam-filled mugs. There were a few empty seats, and, since it was the custom under such circumstances to sit with strangers, who, more often than not, were buried in morning papers or cheap mystery novels, he was already searching for the best place as he stepped into the cafe.

He recognized her immediately. She was seated alone at a tiny table for two at the back of the room near the hallway that led to the toilets. It was a spot he always gravitated toward himself because there was no foot traffic, and an old, bronze coffee roaster obscured the kitchen grill. She was wearing the same jacket and a pastel turtleneck sweater that made her face bright and clean. She was prettier than he had thought.

He shook his coat and walked quickly to the table. He stood a moment, watching her.

"May I sit down?" he asked.

She made a tentative sound, moved her coffee cup and butter croissant, but did not look up. He smiled, arranging himself in the chair.

He could not tell what she was reading. The paperback was flat down on the table. Her brow was furrowed just enough to make him want to wet a finger with his tongue and touch the space between her eyes.

Manny brought him a cup of Costa Rica, his favorite blend, and said, "How you been, Steve? Haven't seen you for awhile."

"Busy," he said.

"Everybody's busy, all right. What'll it be?" Manny knew he was watching the woman and smiled.

"Short stack," he said. "Butter on the side."

Manny nodded, tapped his arm, and walked away.

He watched as she turned one page, then another. He sipped the coffee.

"Well, hello," he said finally.

Her jaw tensed. She hunched a shoulder.

"Remember me?" he asked.

She looked up.

Her eyes were enormous blue lights. Her cheekbones were high, which made her face seem strong and dependable. She had a lovely mouth, with a little dip beneath the center of a straight nose. Under the jacket against the sweater her breasts were quite full, and he guessed that she was self-conscious about them. He was amazed at how, every time in this initial stage, he felt always so thrilled and naive.

She cocked her head and said, "I beg your pardon."

"You were right," he said. He sipped from the mug.

"Was I?" she replied.

She was fairly shut down. It was not wise, therefore, to be clever.

"The weatherman." He smiled. "It's still raining cats and dogs."

It was a delight to see her struggle with recognition, gratitude, and obligation.

"Oh," she said, and made a smile.

She had beautiful white teeth, behind which her tongue darted, as though trying to escape.

"I didn't know you came in here," he said. "I've never seen you before."

"I don't come often," she said. "There's a deli the next block up."

"I've been there," he said.

Manny brought the pancakes, grinned, and backed away.

"My name is Palmer," he said. "Steven Palmer." He held out his hand.

"Elizabeth," she said. "Dickerson."

She took his hand. Her fingers were beautifully tapered, the nails carefully done. It was a good sign.

"Would you like some of this?" he said, pushing the plate a bit.

"Oh, no," she said.

"They have great hotcakes here."

"Yes, I've had them," she said.

"I'm with Highlander and Stirton, downtown," he ventured. "Export, import."

He thought it much the better course to offer information and let the other respond. No one likes being questioned, at least initially.

"I had just come out of my office when I saw you," he continued. "I was lucky myself to get a cab."

"It was a nasty night," she said, closing the book. He could see the title now: *Sense and Sensibility.*

Dead female writers.

"I'm a marketing agent for a wholesale supplier," she finished. "I leave my car there. I was a few days in the country."

He was impressed, as much for his safety as for her progress in the world.

There was that silence now which comes when people realize they know enough to turn back or, possibly, push on to the destination ahead. He chewed his pancakes while she rearranged a few crumbs upon her plate. Manny brought the coffee pot.

"It's supposed to storm all day," he said, when Manny walked away.

"That's what I've heard too," she said.

"Well," he laughed, "now that's the first time we've agreed."

"About what?" she said, her brows closing a bit.

"The weather," he replied.

She laughed. A genuine laugh. Not one of those manufactured things that lets the other know how much you might, after all, tolerate becoming interested.

He faced her. This time she did not lower her eyes.

Manny returned with two tickets and set them carefully upon the table. He grabbed hers.

She said, "Please don't do that."

"Why?" he asked. "Your money's no good with me."

She frowned. "It's presumptuous," she said.

"It doesn't presume anything but kindness and generosity," he returned. "And maybe a bit of old-fashioned male courtesy. There's little enough of that around these days, don't you think?"

"As well as female submissiveness, I suppose."

He narrowed his eyes just enough to be taken seriously. "All those things are really irrelevant," he said. "All that matters are people."

"Really," she said.

"I don't pay attention to such things," he said, tucking her ticket into his pocket. "But if it's important for you to stay even, I have a perfect solution."

"Oh?" she said.

She was enjoying it now, and he could see that she was enjoying it.

"The movie's in town. I've been wanting to see it. You could take us to the movies."

The cab and the breakfast. They were enough to make for sufficient obligation, if he had read the signs correctly.

"I see," she said. "And what movie is that?"

He reached over and tapped the cover of her book.

She smiled. "But I haven't finished it yet."

"What difference does it make?" he said. "They're never the same anyway, are they?"

It seemed the right thing to say, for her face lit up and she laughed again, a delighted, free laugh. He supposed that she was much concerned about levels of reality and could, with some precision, separate them out. As for himself, he hadn't read a novel in three years.

"I simply couldn't see the film before having finished the book."

"Elizabeth," he said, "it's going to rain all day."

At the sound of her name in his mouth, she reddened. He felt a vulnerability so guarded, yet intense, that it was as though she had, quite spontaneously, removed her sweater to let him have a look. He trembled and closed his legs beneath the table.

She was aware too of what had happened, for she saw the slight hitch in his shoulders and felt the movement of his chair. It was one of those moments one looks back upon and remembers long after everything has passed.

She blinked. "All right," she said. "I'll get it done," and gave him the number of her building.

"Whatever we have to eat later, then," he said, "will be on me. Okay?"

In this way a debt would be perpetuated, which, if they played it as they had, might never be repaid. He understood this and believed she understood it as well. The decision to be together, in other words, was anything but casual. He enjoyed validating his knowledge by predicting how things would turn out.

Feeling a bit more triumphant, he rose, while she gathered her things, stood, and buttoned her coat.

"Until six-thirty, Elizabeth," he smiled.

She looked at him, with nothing personal in her glance, just curiosity, as though she had found a new book and were only leafing through the pages.

"Six-thirty, then," she agreed, pulling her collar up and moving away. But she hesitated, recalling something proper, turned, and said, "Steven."

Through that morning and into the early afternoon it rained hard. He kept the television on, watching first a rerun of the Knicks-Lakers game on ESPN and then a special about mountain climbing in Tibet. He imagined her sitting on a print sofa, her feet tucked under her, sipping herbal tea, and reading *Sense and Sensibility.*

He even found himself thinking about his second wife, Arleen, from whom he had been divorced now for eleven months. She had been a good wife, as wives go, faithful and unpretentious and, even, at the end, never angry. She had been so levelheaded and devoted, in fact, that the excitement he had felt the first time he saw her, at the Heatherstones' anniversary party, when she had had a little too much to drink, seemed later, after they were married, to have been a trick. It was true that, whenever they went to bed, a few martinis made things more original, but it troubled him to think that she might be afraid of him. After a time the taste of vermouth before lovemaking upset his stomach, and he wondered what he had ever seen in her. They stayed together, however, for eight years.

He had had affairs, of course. They had nothing to do, he was convinced, with what Arleen and he shared, or didn't share. The penis, he believed, was without conscience, and to this date he had not made up his mind about the corresponding part of a woman's anatomy. He supposed, though, that it was the same. Fairness, certainly, demanded it.

The special about mountain climbing in Tibet was boring, but he left it on, letting his mind descend to the persistent drumming upon the window pane. It made thinking about women easier and evened out any comparisons he made among them.

He had had three relationships since the separation, which had taken place fourteen months before. He thought of them now one by one, the last particularly, Evelyn was her name, who had had enormous brown eyes, a full mouth, and a terrible thing she did with her tongue when they made love, that was all he really seemed to miss about her. He never thought of his first wife, Josie, who had been a complete bitch and had separated him from his youth.

It was not the male thing. He did not believe in the male thing. He needed love, devotion, and happiness as much as the next person. His heart was open to discovery. He believed that every human being was like that, a solitary seeker after an impossible dream. Indeed, sometimes, walking along the street at noon, when the buildings were emptied of all the people, when they all pressed together shoulder to shoulder toward nowhere in common, he thought of them like long-lost family, who could not recognize their mutual heritage, even though they had been born of the same mother. And as to those who appeared to have found some measure of joy, they were either fatuous or stupid, having overlooked, because of their deficiency, the deeper complications of life. They made hope, a remnant of which still played at the back of his mind, seem ironic or unfair. It was when he succumbed to a consideration of this that bitterness entered his heart, and he entertained the conclusion that he would not find the right woman, because no such creature existed. There was only this looking and acquiring, this perpetual coming down from the hills, like a rutting stag, this shopping among those who, like himself, muddled along the streets.

And then, suddenly, at four o'clock, the rain stopped. Something bright entered his rooms. He got up, turned off the television, took the elevator down to the street, and stepped outside.

The sky was blue. Great puffs of white floated beneath it. Everything was shining, sparkling. Across the street the flag above the Espresso Cafe hung limp. People stood about, smiling. He began walking briskly. He went a block, two blocks, then turned. By the time he got back to his building, the clouds had split, dissolving, and people had come out in front of the cafe to sit and drink coffee. He wanted coffee as well, but instead rode the elevator to his apartment and switched on the television. It was a pact of anticipation he was willing to establish with Elizabeth, sequestered in her rooms, flooded by sunshine, hurrying through a novel about dead women.

That night they took a cab uptown to where the movie was playing.

Of course, one does not talk in a movie. And he knew, after the first five minutes, that he did not want to be there. Depictions of men and women, how they get on, how they struggle to be mutually respected, how they search among dreams and fantasies and social restrictions to be joined, how they, in short, love, bored him. Nothing ever truly happened. He only found himself awash in conversation. The notion that any of it might apply to his own life was intrusive. Television was no better, and, aside from a sporting event here and there, he used the VCR and rented the old black-and-whites, which were always direct.

He sat next to her, careful to give up all space on the armrest. From time to time he glanced at her. She sat forward, a bit tense, lips parted, staring intently at the screen. He smiled and tried to imagine how they would be together, six months from now.

When it was done, they sat in the cab, heading to Umberto's, one of his favorite restaurants, and she asked, "What did you think?"

"About what, Elizabeth?"

"The movie, of course."

He faced her and tried to make his voice serious. "Relationships," he replied.

"Yes?" she said.

"It was about relationships."

She cocked her head. The lights from the street made vague shadows across her face. "Relationships," she agreed.

"Was the book better?" he asked.

"Yes," she said. "Much."

"That's always the way, then," he said.

When they were seated at Umberto's and he had pushed the candle to one side, she said, "And expectations."

"What?" he said.

"Expectations. Relationships. *Sense and Sensibility.*"

"Yes," he said. "Do you think it ever possible to get on without them?"

"Expectations?" she replied, rubbing her fingers against the stem of the wine glass. "No."

"I wonder," he said. "Perhaps it is, if you train yourself."

"Train?" she said.

"Through experience. To let things be. To not manipulate them. Like in the movie."

"You were watching, then," she smiled.

"Of course," he said.

"I thought, perhaps, you weren't. That you were just there. For my sake."

He wanted not to lie too much, for the road had smoothed faster than he had planned, but it was not possible. Love had only a superficial acquaintance with truth.

"It was a good movie," he said. "I haven't read the book, though."

"I'll lend it to you," she said.

That's what he wanted to hear. If he chose, it could take him forever to get it done. He felt completely relaxed now. She sat back and rested an elbow on the table. Her eyes were warm.

So he told her about the divorce. Both divorces. He kept any disillusion from his voice because he was not, after all, disillusioned. He was forthright, honest. If there had been failure, there was knowledge.

If he had lost something bright and new, he had found his way in the dark and was better for it. Naturally, he had said all these things before, so that, in a way, he watched himself perform, while at the same time he was in the lobby buying popcorn. You had to fill out the application, didn't you? So he did, precisely, directly, and from the heart. In that way nothing had to be taken from the file later to be reexamined.

She had never married, he was told, as the salad came and went and the entrée arrived, still simmering in olive oil and garlic.

She was thirty-five, from a small town upstate, where her parents had lived and died, bequeathing her a vacation cottage, to which she retreated from time to time, she smiled warmly, to grow roses. She had just come from there, in fact, when he found her that night waiting in the rain.

"Getting over something too," he declared.

She looked into his eyes. "Yes. Something."

"Disappointment, again?"

"Expectations," she agreed.

He felt a rush of freedom. No matter what developed now, he foresaw no trouble. She was a realist as well, accustomed to goodbye. At the same time he experienced an odd sense of commitment or dedication, for hadn't he learned enough not to be judged unworthy, like any other?

So he asked, "Would you ever marry, do you think?"

"I don't know," she said.

"Do you think it's even truly possible?"

"Steven, that I marry?"

"That men and women can do that. Truly."

She laughed. "Of course they can. They do all the time. What makes you ask a question like that? Disappointment, then?"

Her eyes twinkled.

"Well, I mean truly. Without illusions."

"You mean disillusions."

He couldn't help himself. He liked her more than he had expected.

"Maybe it's just the times that make me say that," he said. He did not want her to think any of this was, after all, weakness.

"What times?" she said, filling his glass with wine.

"These times. Everything. Everyone. It's hard to predict."

"But it's always been that way," she said. "It's the board the game is played on."

"The board?" he said.

"How people meet."

She seemed to have risen and taken command of something, he wasn't sure what. He sat back and studied her as she moved the food upon her plate. *Goddamn,* he thought, *she is beautiful.*

And so it began.

He cooked. She cooked. She liked to cycle. They rented bikes. He liked to canoe in the park. They rented canoes. He slept over with her. She slept over with him.

Her place was very pleasant, strewn with flowers, particularly roses, which she undoubtedly carried in from the country. The cushions of her chairs were flowered. There was floral wallpaper in the bathroom and the bedroom. She liked sunny, airy things. The windows stayed open. The curtains blew. The scent of blossoms was everywhere. He liked it very much.

His rooms were spartan by comparison. Danish furniture. Metal lamps. Plain rugs. Framed posters on the walls. Black stereo cabinet. A Sony television on a revolving stand. She enjoyed being there, did not try to change a thing, made no suggestions. She took him for what he was, in other words. As he did her.

It seemed silly after the first few months that they maintain separate quarters. They spoke of it sometimes, jokingly, over breakfast or while driving in her car to the cottage upstate. Why would living together involve any loss of independence, when they enjoyed each other so much? They played with it a little, sleeping a few days in a row at her place or his. When they did that, he found it hard to be alone in his apartment. That was a good sign, he believed, but it troubled him. Best of all, he liked the time they spent at the cottage.

It was a pretty place, set in a stand of pine trees through which a tiny lake shone, like a jewel. They walked there, holding hands.

The cottage had two bedrooms, a small kitchen, and a combination dining room and living area that opened out to a deck. They ate on the deck often, had drinks and talked. Below the deck was the rose garden.

She liked to work there. Every time they visited, something had to be done: pruning, staking, watering, tying up. He stood sometimes on the deck, a drink in his hand, watching her move up and down the rows.

She always wore the same floppy hat and white cotton gloves, and at first he thought it quaint and feminine for her to be devoted to things so delicate and fragile. But as the months passed, the time she consumed gardening, while he fussed alone in the cottage, looking for something to do, began to bother him. He wasn't sure at first just why this was. She could be expected, always, each time they visited, to spend some hours working. The floppy hat. The cotton gloves. The shears with electric tape wrapped around the handles. The dirty sneakers.

She never invited him into the garden. He respected this, of course. It was her garden. But he found himself resenting the hours she spent there. Confused and irritated, he had gone out one evening, a glass in his hand, to walk among her roses, but she saw him, bounced quickly from her knees and ran directly toward him, all ten fingers spread, like nets, to hold him back.

"Steven," she said. "Please."

He hesitated, shrugged, then saw the same frown come between her eyes that he had seen that first morning in the Espresso Cafe. He went into the cottage, made himself a fresh drink, and stood on the deck, looking down at her. He found it odd. There was nothing in himself he would not share. After all the experience, everything he was had been used, in some way or other.

He was disappointed. The weeks had turned into months, the months into almost a year, and here he was, disappointed. She had been better in so many ways; nevertheless, there it was.

He had had chances to have affairs and had deliberately ignored them. He had wanted it to last. He had not thought that it couldn't. He understood now that it must. There had never really been any other possibility.

Perhaps she understood this too, since she was not stupid, and this was the meaning of the garden. Why lose it all, if you thought, in the end, you would lose. She was damned smart.

They made love that night, and, around three o'clock, he awoke to find her naked, standing above him.

"What are you doing?" he asked.

"Looking at you," she said.

"Why?"

"Just fascinated, I guess."

He took that as a pretty good compliment and pulled her down to him.

There was, he believed, no proper way to say goodbye, but, if he had read her correctly, that did not matter. So they went on a few more weeks, a full month, then she suggested another trip to the country.

No proper way, he supposed, but sometimes a right time.

He maintained an even composure. He enjoyed being with her. Perhaps, at times, he still would be, if she were willing.

They had dinner and walked at the lake. The next afternoon she puttered in the garden. Frowning, he watched her from the deck, a drink in his hand. The impulse he felt to crash through her roses amused him.

She came in finally, cleaned up, and they had a couple drinks and together prepared dinner. It was a particularly fine sirloin tip, which they smothered in mushrooms and onions. He ate hungrily and enjoyed the cabernet she poured for him.

When they were done, he produced the novel, set it on the table and said, in a low, even voice, "I thought I had better return this to you."

"I see," she replied, sitting forward. "Did you enjoy it, then?"

"Oh, yes," he said.

Actually, he had not opened it.

"Perhaps you'll let me lend you another sometime."

"I'd like that," he said, filling his chest with air.

"Well," she said, "we're ready for a little brandy, aren't we? Would you do the honors?"

She pointed, produced a key from the pocket of her skirt and handed it to him. He went to the mahogany cabinet, which he had never seen open, relieved that his predictions about her had been so accurate. She was quite sensible.

He bent to unlock the cabinet and put his hand out to steady himself. She waited beside him. He opened the door.

"Inside," she said. "Take your pick."

He looked.

There was the basket she had carried that night in the rain. Beside it was a row of sealed bowls. In each bowl the head of a man floated.

He stood bolt upright, dizzy, clutching his throat.

"The rest," she smiled warmly, "is for the roses."

A House in Order

There could not have been a more appropriate time for John Belden to die. His daughters, Elizabeth and Katherine, were married. His first wife, Evelyn—Evy, she had insisted upon being called—had been killed in a plane crash in the Florida Everglades two years before, having nearly bled him dry with the settlement a decade earlier and several court appearances since. And then Patricia, his second wife, whom he had never truly loved but took on when Evelyn left to keep away the things which appeared at night, had succumbed to an embolism only last winter. The business—he was a dealer in rare tapestries—was prospering. He owed no money. His younger brother Henry, an unrepentant alcoholic for almost thirty years, who had given their mother ceaseless suffering and guilt, had finally, like her, melted into the white nothingness of a convalescent bed, to find, at last, that a shared grave held no memory of the man who had, one black night, deserted them all more than fifty years before.

Appropriate, then, was the word John Belden thought of that morning when Doctor Ames announced that the cancer he had discovered beneath his arm was, in fact, in his neck and shoulder as well, that time was limited, very limited, and he might think about getting his house in order.

He went into the parking lot and lit a cigarette.

He instructed the doctor to keep silent. Suffering, he believed, gains little when shared. Elizabeth and Katherine, who had come to Evelyn and him in moments of forgetfulness, had more than enough to understand concerning their young men, without having to undergo the useless consideration that life, after all, was fortuitous, and that the stranger who had rocked them to sleep in childhood might be so much more than any other old man, when remembered as a father.

But he wanted to tell someone, and so he told Benny Mollenstein, the deaf and dumb proprietor of a corner newsstand where, for years, he had bought his newspapers, magazines, and cigars. A dwarf, Benny read lips, peering above the rows of shining covers, his eyes black stones beneath a veneer of ice.

The stones did not move, but Benny's hands flew up, dancing and jumping across his face and chest. John Belden, after much repetition, had come to comprehend some of these gestures, insofar as they related to prices, the weather or general expressions of friendliness and goodwill. But Benny's hands moved so queerly and quickly now that John Belden stepped back, as though the tiny man had been released from a cage and was trying to get at him.

He stood. The sound of the traffic behind him, which he had known all his life, until it had become a kind of surf, grinding against the city walls, rose in volume and made him look up, to see rectangles of blue fastened to the tops of the buildings.

When he looked down, Benny's arms were at his sides. Tears streamed from his eyes.

John Belden went home to the two-story brownstone he had retained in the settlement with Evelyn. It held the special things he had accumulated over the years, including some of the most precious tapestries. He had placed them with such care that he could not imagine, even now, how they might be otherwise. Often, alone, he walked among them, wondering, as one might in a museum.

Mrs. Hellekson had left his dinner on a covered plate in the oven, for it was Friday, and she had wanted to leave early to visit a sick relative upstate. He ate quietly at the kitchen table and drank two glasses of wine. Then he changed his clothes and walked into the study.

He sat at the polished mahogany desk and opened the bottom drawer with the tiny key he always carried. He removed the metal box and set it before him.

What was there to do? The papers were neatly stuffed into the pockets of a hard brown folder. Will. Deeds. Bank accounts. Broker. Accountant. Lawyer. Lists of assets. Insurance policy. Burial policy.

He closed the box and returned it to the drawer.

A careful and precise man, he had not needed the admonition of a doctor to inform him that a human being was a ledger whose columns must be kept in balance. Addition and subtraction were the mathematics of life. As soon as he could understand, in childhood, the logic of abandonment, he had vowed not to permit anything as ludicrous as the world to shape the bottom line of his soul. That which he could not control he had accepted. Those who wished to leave he had let go. And if, in the end, he must lose even sensibility, the one attribute he might call his own, well, that was fair too. It was a zero-sum game. He had come onto the earth without awareness and would leave it the same way. Nothing plus nothing equals nothing.

He read for awhile, then went upstairs.

The bedroom was quiet. Gone were the bric-a-brac, the chintz and baroque furniture upon which Evelyn had insisted, the flowered paper, satin, lace, and ruffles Patricia had adored. Now the walls were alabaster; the rugs, a pastel rose. The bed covering was textured, pale walnut. The sheets were dove gray. The end tables, the writing desk and love seat were cut from dark pecan. The cushions were ivory beige. Instead of curtains there were interior shutters, a light taupe, with dark pecan accents and rails. Not a pattern or a design anywhere, except over the foot of the bed, against the far wall, where he had hung his most prized possession, a tapestry whose purples, jades, blues, and reds were so intricately interwoven that when he stared at them each night before sleep, they seemed a reality whose fabric could only be measured in a dream.

The next morning he dressed and ate slowly, watching the news on television. The lives of the people on the screen, whether afflicted by disease or betrayal, violence or greed, were as common as squares of concrete in a street. Their suffering was incomprehensible. Their pain, interrupted every few moments by commercials, disappeared beneath the flavors of marmalade and butter. Over the years, while sipping coffee, he had watched populations disintegrate and had learned nothing of his own end. The fact that he must die was no more than another tap upon the remote.

Mrs. Hepper had opened the shop by the time he arrived and was in back, her tiny hands busy about the counters and shelves. Plain but neat, diminutive but untiring, she had come to him twelve years before, after the death of her husband, Ernest, in an automobile crash on the interstate. She had been recommended by a client as faithful and reliable, unlike Ernest, whose marriage to her had been punctuated by one infidelity after another. Even so, that Ernest had died seated beside a young blonde did not prevent Mrs. Hepper from providing him an elaborate funeral at St. Mark's, where, to no one's surprise, she wept uncontrollably. He appreciated such loyalty and rewarded it, though her suffering was as illogical as that of peasant women upon their knees, faces covered by rags, that he saw some-times on the evening news.

A middle-aged woman with faded red hair and makeup as precise as the colors of a mural came into the shop at eleven, wandered about, and left. A gentleman in a tailored black cashmere jacket, powder-gray slacks, organdy shirt, and bow tie stepped in just after lunch and bought a tapestry for five thousand dollars. There were several customers in the early afternoon, and just before closing, Mr. and Mrs. Eggelston, who had, in the last two years, made several pur-chases, found yet another piece to their liking and wrote him a check for eight thousand dollars.

It was that kind of business, which suited his temperament per-fectly. At five o'clock Mrs. Hepper said goodbye, and at five-thirty, as was his way, he took a slow turn through the shop, studying the tap-estries, marveling, as always, at how such intricacy, detail, charm, and poetry, mysteriously held by colored lines of thread, could be so unrelated to the world at large and yet be so much more real than anything else he had ever experienced. Beyond the women he had known, those he had married, the few he had entertained before and since, even his own daughters, they were the single joy he would regret.

At six o'clock he stood before the newsstand watching the tiny man sell his papers. Expressions came to Benny's face like cutouts pinned upon a mask. Always late, they hung a moment, proper, but mismatched to a world that, busy and preoccupied, had come to regard him as a kind of sophisticated apparatus, capable of dispensing change.

When Benny saw him, the face settled about the dark eyes, which took on an incredible brightness. Benny reached into a pocket, produced a small piece of paper and held it out. On the paper was written, Sorry. Sorry. Beneath the words was an address.

John Belden held the piece of paper between his forefinger and thumb. Benny swayed from one foot to the other, nodding. A young woman in a pale orange suit wanted to buy a magazine. She waved the magazine and shouted. Benny continued to nod, his eyes fallen into black holes of ice.

John Belden stared.

The following day no one came into the shop. It was just as well. He wanted to make a more detailed inventory, not only of the tapestries but also of the supplies and equipment. Mrs. Hepper complained of a headache, and he let her go at one. By four he was done and decided to close.

It was Benny's day off. At the stand he bought a paper and two cigars from Nick Marcopolous, an old Greek sailor whose son managed a fast-food restaurant uptown. Nick had lost his left arm in high seas beating around the Horn, and the son, with whom he was not close, had brought Nick to America and put him into a small apartment over a delicatessen on West Seventy-fifth. Nick took long walks, covering sometimes five miles a day, all through the city. The first time he walked by Benny's newsstand, Benny hired him to fill in.

"Benny like my face," Nick had said. "It is an honest face, wouldn't you say so?"

John Belden had nodded.

"Benny not feel sorry for old Nick. I am strong still. You see?" And he had raised the one arm, whose muscle drew tight against the cotton plaid shirt. "Not sorry for Nick, you bet. Smart for Nick. That Benny, he know. Honest, is right? I do anything for that Benny."

The old man had told him the whole story the first day at the job, while Benny stood alongside, gesturing and smiling. After that, the stories were of the sea and the women Nick had loved.

John Belden watched the one good arm dart and stab above the rows of magazines. The old sailor had a trick of tucking a paper against his side and holding it there with the stub of his bad arm. When the customer paid and there was change, Nick dropped the money into the customer's hand, then, with a twist and a turning motion of the stub, threw the paper forward and caught it in his hand, whereupon he delivered it softly into the open palm. Regular customers always paid with bills, in fact, to watch, in delight, the old sailor do his stunt. As far as anyone knew, Nick had never missed.

John Belden lit one of the cigars and held it loosely in his mouth. When he returned the matches to his pocket, his fingers touched the piece of paper.

He held the paper out and looked at it. The word repeated itself. He read the address.

Nick was doing his trick. The newspaper jumped forward, turning once so it could be caught at the fold. The customer, a young man in a double-breasted navy suit and no tie, cried, "You see!" to the woman beside him, who clapped her red-nailed hands and laughed. The young man tossed a coin at Nick. The old man grabbed it easily and saluted. John Belden looked up the street, where the early evening had collected, like sparkling rubbish.

It had been particularly warm that day, but now the air was cool, and he was content to stand to one side, smoke his cigar, and watch the people. He had lived with them all his life, only a step, a shoulder width, a wall away, yet apart. He had found freedom in this, a liberation of the mind for imagined things. To be among strangers but to have their services was as easy to understand as multiplication and division, measured by the currency in his billfold and the statements he received at the end of each month. The pursuit of sensibility rested upon indifference, and he did not begrudge them a thing because his life was ending and they paid no attention.

He watched Nick Marcopolous sell papers. The smile never left Nick's face. His broken English and laughter leapt across the rows of colored magazines, interrupting traffic. He liked the old sailor. He was the perfect substitute for a dwarf who could neither speak nor hear.

John Belden looked down. His hand held the piece of paper.

He began to walk. He walked one block, then another. At the third intersection he stopped, returned to the curb, then stood several minutes, watching the signals change. He hailed a cab and gave the driver the address.

Benny lived on the South Side. The gray building had not been cleaned in years. Writing covered the walls.

The city was quieter here; the surf was a distant murmur beyond stone. John Belden waited, expecting that Benny knew he was there and would come waddling out of the ugly building toward him, stubby hands grabbing and spinning in a hieroglyphic of joy.

A young man with long black hair pulled behind his head and held by a band, sat watching him from the front step. John Belden came forward and stopped.

"I wonder," he said, "if you might help me, please."

The young man looked at him and did not blink.

"I want to see someone," he said. "In there." He pointed at the building. "Do you live there?"

The young man moved something inside his mouth. John Belden took out his wallet. "I would pay you. He can't hear. Mr. Mollenstein."

"Mollenstein," the voice came, peculiarly high, higher on the second syllable. "The runt."

John Belden offered a bill. The young man took it, turned it over, shrugged, then disappeared. In a few moments he returned, jerked his thumb backward and said, "Second floor, rear."

John Belden climbed the steps and opened the door.

The first thing that struck him was the smell: stale, fried meat, tobacco, and dust. Then it was the light, as though a woolen blanket had been thrown over the building. He climbed slowly, being careful to stay in the center of the stairs. At the end of the long corridor a door was open. The tiny man stood there, one hand flipping and turning against his face.

John Belden stood directly before the dwarf and said, "Benny." He held up the piece of paper.

Benny moved aside. John Belden walked into the room.

It was a small room, made smaller by a curtain tacked to the ceiling at one end. The walls were covered by photographs, mostly of women from the covers of old magazines. Magazines and newspapers were stacked upon the floor. A small sink and hot plate were at the other end of the room. In the center of the room were cushioned chairs between which rested an old nightstand. Upon the nightstand was a large black-and-white photograph of a man and woman in a turn-of-the-century pose. The man, his eyes enormous circles of black liquid, stood behind the woman, who was seated. Next to the photograph was a letter-size carbon slate of the kind children once used to practice their alphabet. What looked to be a new television sat just in front of the two chairs. The television was on, but there was no sound.

Benny gestured to one of the chairs and switched off the set. He picked up the slate, produced a piece of chalk, and wrote, Drink?

John Belden nodded.

Benny wrote, What?

He shook his head and raised his shoulders. "Whatever you have."

Benny smiled, shuffled to the refrigerator, which was no larger than a medicine cabinet, and produced a glass milk bottle, which contained an amber liquid. He filled two glasses, returned, handed him one, then propped himself in the other chair.

John Belden drank. The liquid was sweet, a mixture of fruit juice and a long, warm flavor at the end.

Rum, Benny wrote across the slate.

John Belden smiled and drank again.

They sat. He was confused and a bit ashamed because he did not understand why he had come. Yet he was comfortable, in spite of the room and the strangeness of the tiny man, separated from his newsstand. He could appreciate a life out of which freedom had been woven from total silence.

Benny looked at him and picked up the slate.

He wrote, No work today?

John Belden faced him. "Yes," he said. "Closed early. Tired."

Benny wrote, Tired. Yes.

John Belden put his head back against the cushion of the chair. He looked at the ceiling, which was as nondescript as the sidewalk outside. He closed his eyes.

He did not hear the small man move, but when he sat forward, Benny was standing by the chair, staring at him.

Benny wrote, What you do?

John Belden said, "You mean, work?"

Benny smiled, then nodded.

He could not think of what to say. How could what he had given his life to be contained in a few words a deaf-mute might comprehend?

So he said, "Benny, would you like to see?"

Benny nodded.

"Your next time off, then, I'll show you."

Benny studied him carefully, then returned to his chair.

John Belden's eyes fell upon the black-and-white photograph. He reached over and tapped it.

"Benny," he said. "Yours?"

Benny nodded. His eyes became fixed upon the old picture. John Belden took the slate, rubbed his hand across it and wrote, Alive?

He held out the slate. Benny took it. He studied the word. He looked at John Belden, his round, dark eyes floating to the surface of his face. He rubbed the slate and wrote, Mother, no. Father, yes. Then, beneath, one more word: You?

Benny watched his mouth when he said, "Mother, no. Father." But his eyes drifted. He turned. Benny leaned from the chair, a stuffed toy trying to stand.

Somewhere his father, perhaps, lived, or lay buried, mourned, when memory served, by strangers who did not know that he, John Belden, a sole survivor, was also worthy of pity.

When he looked back, Benny's face wore an expression as intricate as any he might have imagined. He could not bear to decipher it, deep in the logarithms of his heart. He seized the slate and scrawled, Don't know.

Benny read the words. He looked at John Belden, then pointed to the grimy window that looked out to the world below. He slapped his chest and pointed again. He formed the word with his lips.

John Belden nodded and shut his eyes.

Benny took the slate and wrote it: Sorry. Sorry.

The following week, mouth open, stubby fingers locked together, Benny moved carefully from tapestry to tapestry. Standing to one side, in the twilight which always descended near closing, John Belden saw the colors reflected upon the surface of Benny's eyes, beneath which still shone a dark ice.

It was a moment when amusement gave way to something profound.

So specialized was what he had to offer that only those with some awareness dared browse through his shop. The tapestries, detailed, involved, subtle, and complex, were an intellectual exercise. To look at them demanded an ordering of the mind. This mute little man was a rag doll pressed up against a window.

Yet, watching Benny's eyes, John Belden was struck by the quality of the moment. He had always thought that between knowledge and speech lay a barrier that could not be overcome. Life was incomprehensible; silence, the stuff out of which all things were made. Art was piecework for the damned.

This logic was perfectly demonstrated when, at the end of the tour, Benny produced his slate and scribbled one word: Pretty.

John Belden stood beside the dwarf. He tried to find this simple judgment written in the delicately colored thread. It was ludicrous. He was embarrassed. Something which seemed so real could exist only in the deepest reaches of the soul. Even those who bought the tapestries were fools. He had never felt so alone.

The next day he closed early. At the newsstand he bought a cigar. Benny handed him a piece of paper on which was written, I show you now.

That Friday, Benny arranged for Nick to come in and was waiting behind the counter when John Belden arrived. Benny wore a herringbone jacket whose lapels were too wide, a blue button-down shirt with frayed collar, and a loosely knotted foulard tie that might have been used years before by a ten-year-old boy attending Sunday school. In one hand he held a small bunch of yellow flowers. In the other was the slate chalkboard.

Nick was doing his stunt. The newspaper flew out from beneath the stub, turned over once and was caught by the good hand, like an escaping bird. Nick laughed, was thrown a tip, danced a tight jig above the bright magazine covers and, winking at John Belden, cried, "Wouldn't you say so?"

Benny took him on the bus to a part of the city he had only seen from the tops of very tall buildings. Squat, block-long structures. Masonry bunkers. Pink tenements stacked against each other like dominoes. Barred windows. Doors with grilles. Traffic signals blinking above empty streets.

They went into a gray, five-story box and walked down a long corridor that smelled of Lysol. Benny held the flowers and chalkboard to his chest, staring straight ahead. John Belden kept his hands in his pockets.

At the end of the corridor was a marble-top desk. A flat-nosed woman in a white, starched uniform wrote on a clipboard when they passed.

Making one turn after another, Benny took him so far into the building that he became lost. Doors lined the halls. Numbers were impaled upon them. Some of the doors were open. He could see narrow beds in rows. In the beds were people so old they were like fossils removed from caves. The smell of antiseptic was not strong enough here.

They went into a small room partitioned by a curtain. On one side of the curtain was an unmade bed. On the other side lay the oldest man John Belden had ever seen.

The man's eyes, immense black discs, were open, staring at the ceiling. The mouth formed a perfect, narrow circle, through which air escaped and was caught. The face, deeply lined, had not been shaved in days. The head was completely bald and the color of newspaper that has been left in the rain.

Benny placed the yellow flowers into a porcelain vase. He went to the bed, his eyes only slightly above those of the old man.

Then a thing happened which so frightened John Belden that he wanted to run from the room, through the corridors, until he reached the street below.

Benny put both hands flat against the bed, gave an odd twist to his stunted body and flopped up beside the old man. He crawled, took the naked head in his arms, his fingers tapping and touching, and began to rock, a rag doll with a toy too big to hold.

As Benny rocked, tears filled his eyes. His tiny body shook. The old man's head went back and forth, but nothing on the old man moved, not even the eyes, which were round and still.

John Belden heard a sound. He was not sure that it came from Benny or the old man or both together, but it was like no other sound, so inarticulate, so animallike that it surely must have been exhumed from that same ancient cave.

He stood, terrified. The sound held, resonating at the back of his teeth. Then Benny stopped, placed the bald head against the pillow and climbed from the bed.

Benny watched the old man. John Belden waited. The silence was absolute. Benny picked up the slate, produced a piece of chalk and bent forward. He held out the slate. It read, Father. Hopeless.

John Belden could not bear to speak, so he erased the slate and wrote, Sorry. Sorry.

The following day he kept the blinds closed in the shop until well after noon. The colors of the tapestries blurred and ran together. A few people tried to peer in then walked away. He would not close, but he did not want to see anyone. Mrs. Hepper talked to a middle-aged couple and then the curator of the Whitman Museum, who came in after three. At five o'clock he locked the door.

He went to the newsstand. Benny was selling papers, his arms and hands moving in that language no one understood. When Benny saw him, he stopped abruptly and nodded. He would not stop nodding.

When John Belden bought a cigar, Benny pressed a piece of paper against his hand. He folded the paper into his pocket.

He did not read it when he got home. He did not read it while he ate dinner. He did not read it when Mrs. Hellekson closed the front door behind her. He read it after he had dressed for bed and sat alone under the single lamp in the study. Then he went upstairs.

A week passed before he stood at Benny's newsstand. Doctor Ames had looked again, had consulted others, looked some more, prescribed drugs, but there was no light in the doctor's eyes.

John Belden stared at the dwarf.

The next day they rode the bus to the gray building. Benny led him to the room where the old man lay. He closed the door into the hallway.

John Belden stood to one side as Benny crawled up onto the bed and took the old head in his arms. He rocked slowly, tapping and touching. He rocked for a very long time, until everything in the room seemed to move, and John Belden felt the marrow of his life, tapping and touching.

Then Benny stopped. John Belden went to the side of the bed. Benny nodded. He did not look up. He nodded, nodded. John Belden heard his heart beating.

He stared at the old man and then at Benny. Benny lowered the head slowly. He put one stubby hand upon each shoulder.

John Belden took the pillow and placed it over the grizzled face.

He could not fault the logic of the dwarf. Even art, at the end, gives way to the essential. Terminating the existence of something which had no awareness, yet lived anyway, was perfectly measured by the disease eating his own life. He summoned his strength and leaned forward. His arms trembled. His hands rang.

Then the strangest thing happened. He looked at Benny, who was sobbing. Upon his face joy, gratitude, terror, pity, and awe were woven into the most intricate pattern he had ever seen.

And in that moment he wanted desperately for it all to return, everything, again and again, because there was no way to comprehend finality, and he was not meant to die.

Vital Statistics

I was glad when the divorce was done. Kathryn took care of it. Over the months I hadn't appeared before the judge or even consulted a lawyer. I didn't protest anything. Once in a while pieces of carbon tissue arrived from a place called Bennett, Bennett and Shaw. I put the tissues into a bottom drawer of my desk. It was like getting billed by American Express.

It bothered me when the names appeared in the paper. There was an entire list of us, in fact—strangers, arranged alphabetically under Petitions for Dissolution. They also had lists for Births, Deaths, Marriages, and Final Decrees. Recently they added Bankruptcies. I have become addicted to these lists and read them faithfully.

I moved into an apartment in town, and Kathryn kept the place in the country. I didn't like that. I've always needed room and despised the press of city life. People clutter up intersections and elevators. I'm always stepping around them or almost bumping into them. It's impossible to walk in a straight line. Everyplace is like a restaurant or movie theater. You can't hear anything distinctly unless it rises above the general din, and the telephones are always warm.

In the country you can hear one thing at a time, like a train crossing an open field far away or a dog barking down the road. If I play it right, though, I may still get the house. Kathryn has always preferred the city.

I didn't really want to see her again. It wasn't hate or bitterness or even anger. I simply did not want to see her. There was nothing to talk about, since I had given it all away to escape, and though I did not blame her or myself, there was responsibility, and when we were together, I couldn't help thinking about it, and I wanted to be washed of the whole thing.

Sometimes we had to talk, however, and she came to the apartment and sat in one of the swivel chairs I had bought at Conrad's. On the day before she went to court for the grand finale, she brought some papers for me to sign.

She had lightened her hair and taken to wearing it pulled to one side, which was most unflattering, in my opinion. She had gotten the idea, I knew, from the group she had begun attending six months before we separated, and when she told me she was dating her therapist "seriously," as she put it, I felt relieved and ashamed. I knew, then, that it was only a matter of time before I got the house, but I felt I had failed, in some deep place I did not understand, as a man.

I was pretty much of a recluse in those days. I would hang around the apartment, which was actually quite comfortable; it was high enough to have a good view of the lake, and I enjoyed watching the boats at sunset and reading. I also like my work and don't mind taking it home, though I am at a place in the firm that makes even conscientiousness unnecessary. There were a couple of small restaurants where I had become known, a little Italian place that didn't open until six and a Mexican cafe, where I used my college Spanish so well that one of the waiters always greeted me with "mi querido amigo."

But then, two weeks later, when the final decree appeared among the lists, I felt terribly alone and knew that something had to be done.

The thought of sitting at bars unnerved me. Going to dinner with Kathryn or stopping with Jerry Crampton or Bill Upham after work at a darkened booth, I had spent hours studying men with gray at the temples, their silk shirts open to the second button and rings on the third and fourth fingers of their right hands. They wore Vuarnets, drove white Corvettes or black Targas, and lived in apartments with metal furniture.

The women were scary as well. They wore too much makeup. Their calves were muscled from aerobics or, worse yet, from running in the park at dawn. Though they were over thirty, nearly forty, they tried to look like something out of *Seventeen,* and they combed their hair oddly, like the lead singer of last year's rock group.

They were all divorced, separated, or on the way, and they appeared wealthy, in a kind of glitzy fashion. But I suspected them, and one night Bill pointed out his son's high school PE teacher drooling over an exotic blonde in a backless dress. The truly wealthy, I concluded, have their places, and they're always private.

Bill introduced me to his cousin from upstate. She owned a sweet face, a slight lisp, attended community college at night and had a ten-year-old kid. We went to a spaghetti joint downtown and talked about divorce and Maslow's Hierarchy of Needs. I was terribly embarrassed because, except for the obvious physical heat that passes between a male and female, which only makes me feel like a tomcat prowling backyards—my brother Frank calls it, affectionately, The Hunt—it was as though I were fifteen again. I had forgotten everything I ever understood concerning women, so I told her—a complete stranger—all about myself. Even while I spoke, I realized, stupidly, that it was a plea for mercy, and when I saw the look of relief on her face, I knew why monogamy is the curse of mankind. She slept with me that night, but I could not remember her name in the morning.

Jerry tried to get me into the singles group he had joined after his divorce from Margaret.

"That's where I met Irene," he said. "Everybody's loose and friendly. It's easy to meet people. You'll have a great time. You'll see. The people are mature. They're actual people."

That was risky enough, since I hadn't met many actual people in my life—mostly they were sort of people—but when I stood at the door on a bleak November night, I felt foolish. I was admitting defeat, wasn't I, going to a place like this? Wasn't it only a cut above having a dating service set you up? A failure of the heart, that's what I was. A wallflower of love.

I stood on the threshold with a fishhook in my back, and the only thing that tore me free and into the room was the image of all those Targas and Corvettes lined up in the garage at the Colony Club.

There are experiences that put a seal on things. They let you know that one part of your life is finished so that another can begin. Graduations and weddings are like that. Mustering out of the army, being fired or released from prison. A door closes behind you, and the light blinds your eyes.

It was a big room, like something attached to a church. On a table near the door were a large coffee urn and styrofoam cups. There were lavender cardboard trays filled with maple bars and glazed do-nuts and an open cigar box stuffed with dollar bills. On the other side of the room was a wet bar.

There was a jukebox, a genuine one, with colored water bubbling along the sides. The music, however, came from a cheap stereo. Tables and folding chairs were set along the walls. People were playing cards and drinking. There were couples on the floor dancing. As I entered, I felt a little shock, as the faces, one by one, turned to regard me with longing or distrust. I backed out slowly and went home.

The following day the final decree appeared among the lists, and I was sure everyone I knew had snipped it from the paper. I decided to spend time alone. What I was experiencing, I knew, was not a prob-lem with women, though, of course, it was.

I began to read in earnest. As an undergraduate I had had a pas-sion for devouring a writer's collected works. I'm the only person I know, for example, who has read the novels of George Bernard Shaw. I had the delusion that I could consume every writer of importance, and there was a time there when I kept ten books going at once.

In addition, I assigned myself tasks, like going to museums or movies. I walked the streets. I watched the sun set every evening for a week. There was something I had missed along the way, something I hadn't learned.

One evening a few weeks later, I was sitting at home reading my lists when I heard a sound at the door. It was not a knock, not distinctly anyway. It was as though an open hand had been placed on the door several times, softly, and removed. I stood up, just a little apprehensive. There had been a rash of burglaries in the neighborhood, and even old man Sexton, who lived in the apartment next to mine and has a license to carry a gun, was more nervous than usual.

I looked at the strange, myopic world of the hallway through the peephole in the door. Nothing. I opened the door carefully (the assassin might be pressed to the wall, a butcher knife clutched against his filthy chest). There was no one. I frowned. Such things, like the calls you get in the night when the other end just hangs up, annoy me. I had begun to close the door when I noticed an envelope lying on the threshold.

I felt my neck hair shiver—you know the feeling—and looked up and down the hallway. The elevator was a couple doors away and across. The little squares with the numbers were dim. There was a stairwell at the other end of the hall.

I looked at the envelope. It was letter size, plain and white. I picked it up and closed the door.

I went back to the leather chair under the lamp and sat down. I held the envelope to the light. Then I tore open one end. Inside was a note written neatly on a single sheet of twenty-weight paper.

Dear Bob,
I saw your name in the divorce column and was surprised. It always seemed to me, when we knew each other, that you were a rather straightforward, stick-to-it kind of man, you know, someone who didn't like defeat, no matter how small the contest. I'm sorry, of course. Such painful experiences are not easy to bear. Believe me, I understand. Perhaps, though, this is a good thing for you. I have learned that pain is a great teacher, even if this sounds a bit sophomoric. It is the only thing that helps us learn the final truths. You see, I'm not so silly as you once thought.
Love,
An Old Friend

I went to the door again, opened it, and scanned the hallway. I returned, sat down, and read the note through several times. Then I went to the window.

The water around the edge of the lake was filled with crystal. The light spread out in ribbons from the shore, but the buildings above them were just so high, and finally the ribbons trailed away and left a vast, shimmering black pond above which there was only darkness.

The emotion I experienced was very curious. It was as though someone had rummaged through my closet while I was reading or had opened my desk drawer and played with my pipe cleaners and stamps. You couldn't get into the building without a key, and this time of night Jack Firestone was at his desk doing crosswords. Someone had deliberately tampered with my privacy and gotten away with it. The fact that it was a woman, a woman that I had once known and impressed in some way, kept me from becoming angry. That and the way it was handled.

I went to bed and fell immediately to sleep. But I came awake at three a.m. and could not drift off again. At three-thirty I got up and went into the living room and read the note. Then I lit my pipe and went over to the window. Except for a streak here and there, the lake was virtually black. A few lights crawled along the lakeshore drive, leading poor souls, exhausted at last and wrung from life, to a fitful rest.

I finished my pipe, washed my face and went to bed. I lay awake until five.

The day dawned clear and fair, and only a light wind blew across the water from the north. I went down in the elevator and caught myself looking for some sign of my nocturnal visitor. I felt foolish. Jack was already gone.

I don't mind the office anymore and move through it with a fair amount of detachment. I went to Rustigian's for lunch with Jerry, and he told me about his sister-in-law, who had just separated from her husband.

"You're turning into a hermit, Bobby," he said, rolling the stroganoff in his mouth. "It's not good for you. You need to get out. Circulate."

"What am I," I smiled, "a garden hose?"

"It's not good for a guy your age to be holed up."

"I'm not holed up."

"What do you call it, then?"

"Tactical withdrawal."

That night I decided not to go out for dinner. I fixed a ham-and-cheese sandwich and settled down to watch Dan Rather and an early movie.

The phone rang. I picked it up, but there was nobody there. I slammed the receiver onto the cradle and went back to my sandwich. The phone rang again.

This time I let a few choice epithets fly. Then I stopped. I heard an intake of breath.

"Who is it?" I asked.

Then something clicked. I can't explain how I knew. Perhaps it was that I had taken the note from my coat pocket many times during the day. There must have been a sympathetic current in the telephone wire.

"It's you," I said.

There was no answer, and I set the receiver on the counter. I stepped to the front door and paused. My heart was racing. I opened the door, and on the threshold was a white envelope. I picked it up and returned to the phone. She had hung up.

I bolted for the door and ran to the elevator. It seemed to take an hour for the car to get to the lobby. I hurried to the desk, where Jack Firestone was doing crosswords.

"Hello, Mr. Carstairs," he said, looking up.

"Jack, did a woman come through here just a bit ago?"

"A lot of women come through here," he said. "What's a six-letter word meaning to show anger or fear? Rhymes with idle."

"You wouldn't have known her," I said. "She would be a total stranger."

"I get lots of those too. Do you know the word, Mr. Carstairs?"

"She might have come in and then gone back out almost immediately, say in just the amount of time it would have taken to ride the elevator up and down."

"No, I can't remember anyone like that. But then I don't look up every time someone leaves. Just when they come in."

Perhaps she was clever, like a terrorist, and had ridden the elevator to the floor above mine, smoked a cigarette and then walked down the flight of stairs to deliver her white letter bomb to my door.

"Thanks anyway, Jack," I said.

"How about the word, Mr. Carstairs? Any idea?"

I put my hand on the envelope in my pocket. "Bridle," I said, and walked to the elevator.

I waited until I got back to the apartment. I went into the kitchen and finished the sandwich. I drank a glass of milk. Then I walked into the living room and sat down.

I tore open the envelope, and there was the handwriting on a piece of twenty-weight paper.

Dear Bob,
You must have wondered about me. I'm sorry I can't say more. I simply can't tell you who I am. I cannot. That's all. It's irrational, I know. Even bizarre. Maybe even crazy. But I know I'm not crazy. Not really. It's only life that becomes crazy, while all the time we stay quite sane. I would like to see you, but from a distance. If you could entertain a fantastic notion, do you know Beldo's on West Kensington? It's quite a large place but very friendly. Will you go there tomorrow evening, say around 7:30?

I was astonished. And frightened. I studied the handwriting. The letters were evenly spaced. The words moved gracefully across the page. Her script was lovely and quite feminine, with nice loops and whirls.

I felt stupid. I stared at my hands. They were sweating.

I went to the window. The darkness across the lake had an eerie quality I had not noticed before. There was no depth to it. Ribbons of light fluttered near the shore, but far across the water there was no light at all, nothing, only the darkness like a great black hole into which everything disappeared.

I wrote down the names of every woman I had ever made love to.

For someone past forty, such a task was not easy. The longer you live, it seems, the more they become one, if only the last one, and I found myself thinking about things I hadn't thought about for years. There were some two dozen of them, and I could not remember all the names, so in a few cases I put down visual clues, like "The Irish Setter" or "Breasts the Size of Baseballs."

I looked at the list and tried to manufacture personalities. Could it be this one? I wondered. Or that one? But I found myself remembering how they had all looked without clothes and what they had done, and I felt sensually but morbidly old. I dozed off and found myself surrounded by them. They all had the time of the relationship written on them. Eight months. A year. Two years. They looked at me and waved. Then there was Kathryn staring at me. She had twelve years printed on her back. I woke, read the note over several more times, and switched on the television.

The following night I was at Beldo's at seven o'clock. I had bought a new camel hair coat the week before, and I wore that, with black wool slacks, a white dress shirt, and a black tie.

I was overdressed, of course. Beldo's is not that kind of place. It reminds me a lot of Lefty O'Doul's in San Francisco. Old wooden floors, a polished, dimly lit bar, and framed black-and-white pictures of dead baseball players on the walls. It was cafeteria style, like O'Doul's, with booths along the sides and tables crowded into the middle. There was even an upstairs. It had been a chic place thirty years ago, but the chic didn't go there anymore.

I sat at the bar and looked around. I hadn't been there myself in five years, and all the help had changed. I recognized no one. Whoever it was, though, I would know her as soon as I saw her, I was sure of it, and I wanted to spot her when she walked in.

She never did. I waited until eight o'clock and then eight-thirty. I got angry and depressed and a bit tipsy. There are just so many gin and tonics one can consume on an empty stomach. So finally I stood in line for a hot roast beef sandwich and coleslaw, and then I went home.

I do not like mysteries, and I imagine that's why I am not religious. The thought of forces lurking beyond that weigh and judge us has always struck me as unfair and capricious. It's hard enough getting through this life without mucking it up with the next.

I left for work late the following morning and had breakfast at Flag's. It's one of those places tourists never discover because it closes after lunch. The breakfast menu has two dozen omelettes and eight different waffles, and the coffee is the best in town. I lingered over a third cup and studied the vital statistics. By the time I got to the office, I was on a pretty even keel.

But there on my desk, propped against the pipe rack, was a plain white envelope. My hand trembled when I touched it.

I buzzed my secretary. "Mary, who brought this letter?"

"It was special delivery, Mr. Carstairs."

"Did a messenger bring it?"

"No, sir. An old man came into the office and handed it to me. He said it was important and that you should have it right away."

She had paid someone off the street to deliver it. "Thank you, Mary."

I left the envelope on the desk and walked to the window. The view from my office is one of the reasons why I dislike the city. Crowded streets, tarred rooftops, and sunlight smeared against glary windows.

I sat down and opened the letter.

Dear Bob,

Thank you for being so trustworthy. Whatever age does to us, it has done to you most kindly. You looked quite handsome in that beautiful jacket. It was such a delight to see you again after all this time. Isn't Beldo's a quaint old place? I'm sorry I ever left it. I'm sorry too that you had to eat your roast beef alone. If it's any consolation, my dinner grew cold on the plate. Enclosed find a ticket to the new play at the Bradley Friday night. I hope you can go.

Love

I couldn't believe it. She had been there the entire time.

Oddly, I was not angry. I was not even depressed at having missed her. I was sad. I read the letter again. She—whoever she was—suffered more than I.

Thus began a series of meetings that were not meetings at all, but adventures, the like of which neither I nor anyone else had ever encountered.

I went to the Bradley, of course. It's a small theater on the South Side that does avant-garde things by young playwrights who don't shave. This one was about a girl from the country seduced and abandoned in the big city. She was pregnant by someone who never appeared but whose presence was always felt, like a kind of "deus mysteriosus," and she lived with an old Mexican who had been with Cesar Chavez in Bakersfield and was disillusioned. The girl felt her life was a useless mess, but she wanted everything for the baby, because it was the only thing she had truly loved. This touched the Mexican, since his son had been killed in a skirmish in a lettuce field. He wanted to take the girl someplace safe and pure, but he was dying slowly from having inhaled too much insecticide. She thought the son should lead the movement to save the world when he was born, for this was, she felt, the best part of the man who had abandoned her, a Vietnam veteran with no left hand. Despair, failure, anguish, and longing. Tennessee Williams with acne.

I looked the house over. At intermission I strolled about the lobby studying each woman's face. I walked up and down every aisle. I found myself catching glimpses of things I thought I recognized, eyebrows here, a nose or cheekbone there, the way a head turned or an arm lay along a wooden seat. She was hiding again. Maybe she was even backstage. I thought about leaving, but decided that wouldn't be fair, to her or the playwright.

The girl died in childbirth, and the Mexican adopted the son.

Cards began coming in the mail. One week a card arrived every day. They were the kind with funny little animals and clever sayings, like, "It's nice to know you're always around," and there would be a gray elephant on a trapeze swinging into the arms of another, or one with a bland, blue little cat being chased by a mutty dog with a pink collar and black nose and the caption, "Ours is a classic relationship." Sometimes tickets came with the cards.

I found myself attending volleyball games, badminton tournaments, and platform-diving championships. I watched the shooting of a detective movie on location and the dedication of a new thirty-story building by the son of the Irish immigrant who had bought the land. I ate dinner at a half dozen neighborhood restaurants I had never heard of, though I have lived in and out of the city all my life. I paid for nothing, but I did not feel guilty, because I thoroughly enjoyed myself, which was totally unexpected. I had a patroness with eyes unlike my own, yet we were strangely compatible.

I struggled against it at first. The acceptance, I mean. That was natural. Every place we "went" I searched frantically for some sign of her. I carried binoculars and watched the stands. I badgered ticket sellers about reservations. I walked through stadiums, parking lots, and stations. I waited outside restrooms.

I even called two names on my list of former lovers, the least remembered and the least gratifying: Carolyn Bally and Pat Thompkins. I ran them down through old friends. They were both married.

"Did you send the letters?" I asked.

They said I was crazy, but they knew of the divorce.

At a modern art exhibit I saw a woman who strangely attracted me. It was the way her hips moved, I think. I followed her from room to room. She looked back at me nervously. Her chin seemed familiar, as though I had once touched it. Her hair was cut across her face, like a helmet. I wanted to cradle her head in my arms.

She paused before the splashes of color framed upon the walls, turning her head this way and that. I felt a little madness come over me. I went up and stood next to her and turned my head this way and that. She looked at me and smiled. She walked quickly into another room and I followed. Her skin was like cream in firelight. I knew I had never seen her before, but I was thoroughly convinced she was the one. She was beautiful, full of passion and joy, and I had always wanted her.

She walked briskly toward a guard in a green uniform and I stopped. She turned to look at me once more, meaningfully, then stepped into an adjacent room. I went out the main entrance and waited.

I waited forty-five minutes before she came out. I had it all planned what I would say.

"Would you like to see a table tennis tournament? Perhaps you'd care for dinner at a little Hungarian restaurant across town? Would you enjoy a Buster Keaton film festival?"

She stopped and looked at me with fear.

"Will you?" I wanted to say. "Will you just please pretend to be the one?"

But I heard my name called, and when I looked back, she was gone.

It was Jerry, wife in tow.

"Glad to see you out, Kid," he said. "This is just the very kind of thing you need."

"Hello, Jerry," I said, looking at his new wife, who was rather mousey but pleasant.

"Yessir, the very thing. He who expands his mind never lives alone."

"Confucius?" I said.

"No, Crampton."

And that's when I was struck with a desperate idea.

Jerry and I were about the same size. When the next invitation and ticket arrived, I dressed him in my trench coat and blue pinstripe, and I went to a novelty shop and bought a make-up kit.

I decided on an old man, with gray hair and beard. I bought a black fedora, rented a cape, and wore my tuxedo. I carried a silver-headed walking stick shaped like an acorn, stooped over a bit and resurrected my foray upon the boards of college theater. I felt absurd but oddly free.

It was a dog show. Jerry sat in my seat, a cap pulled forward on his head, and I prowled through the hall, limping slightly, like the Phantom of the Opera. Between wizened cheeks and powdered brows, my eyes burned like coals. Nothing escaped me. I was a fiend of curiosity. I lurked behind cages. I huddled in corners. I watched every woman who was under fifty. I felt exultant, invisible. This time I would have her. She could not escape.

And she didn't. Only forty minutes after I had begun, I saw a tall, slender figure standing quite still, out of the line of sight of the judges' area, staring intently at the man in the trench coat and gray cap.

I had come up behind her. I could not see her face, but it was she. I had the same feeling I had had that night when she called.

I stood suddenly erect, filled with elation, and threw off my cape.

There was a sound, several sounds, a general surf of sound that broke toward her. My instant rejuvenation had startled the people near me. I saw her turn slightly, the wide brim of her hat lift just enough. There was the line of a white chin, the glint of a dark eye. She put a hand to her face, spun about and broke for the exit.

"Wait," I pleaded. "Please wait."

I began to run. I could have caught her easily, but I stopped. There was something about her flight that was almost hysterical.

The next morning the letter came. It was so strangely painful and frightened that I decided never to trick her again.

She forgave me, and we went on, always separate, and I never recognized, among all the faces, who it could be. We settled into a companionship of untouched life, like two deaf-mutes in parallel universes. I always knew she was there because she told me what I was wearing or mentioned something I had done. Her loneliness was so great that it overcame my own, and one night, in the middle of an Audubon slide show about the Yukon, I stood up and shouted, "Listen, it's all right!" Everyone stared. "Listen!" I repeated. The lecturer, a gray-haired old man with a handlebar moustache, broke into a raucous laugh. "It's all right!" I yelled, spinning around like a dervish, "I love you! I love you!"

Then, smiling, I sat down. I didn't feel like a fool at all.

And that was the end.

The letters stopped. I grew frantic, thinking I had done something wrong. I stayed home from work, hoping there might be a call. I spent hours staring at the lake. I missed her terribly and realized that somehow everything had been quite perfect. We never met or talked, yet, by intention, we were always in the same room, seeing the same things and sharing life together. It was a proper relationship for our time and place.

Then the name appeared in the paper, and I was stunned. I hadn't gone back far enough. It had been that first semester at the university when I had rushed a fraternity and been turned down. She was the girl in the lit class I had dated a few times, never seduced, and completely forgotten. She had become prominent socially and had married several times.

Anne Charles. Her name on that list affected me more than would have divorces from a dozen Kathryns.

I thumbed through the paper. There was the article. She had been ill, quite ill. She had played it this way, I decided, because she had fouled up everything else, and there was no more time. I didn't blame her. I would have done it the same way. A white envelope came in the mail a week later, but I destroyed it.

I've decided to travel. I want to take a long ocean voyage. I want to see the old, old world. Istanbul. Damascus. Cairo. Nairobi. I want to find a place in the desert and dig for bones. I want to uncover the skull of a man who lived a million years ago and hold it in my hands.

Monkey

Monkey Wertzner lived above Heimer's Garage. Each night after work he poured detergent over both hands, kneaded them carefully, rubbed them along each hairy arm until the flesh shone, used but one rag from the five-gallon pail to get everything dry, then went upstairs and turned the burner on under the morning coffee.

Sometimes he looked right away at the photograph taped to the old refrigerator Bill Heimer had given him when Frank Heimer died and Bill had to unload everything from the two-bedroom house on E Street. In fact, Bill had said, "Monkey, why don't you stay in the old man's place? All you have to do is mow the lawn. Rent free. What do you say?" But the room over the garage that Frank had added all that time ago because he didn't care to go home every night to Madge, Bill's stepmother, was fine. Monkey didn't need much.

This evening he looked at the photograph. It was of a young woman, maybe seventeen or eighteen, naked, hands on hips, legs apart, staring straight at the camera, hair pulled to both sides over the shoulders and just touching the breasts, which were quite small. The picture was not from one of those magazines kept behind the register at the Hurry and Go across the street. It was a black-and-white snapped in a backyard somewhere many years before. It had been at the bottom of a cardboard box in the room next to his, where the cartons of oil and parts were kept. Monkey found it the first week he went to work.

Monkey held up his arms, as he always did when he looked. The arms were white. He put them on each side of the picture and bent close.

He opened the refrigerator and removed the tuna casserole he had made the week before. He put two large spoonfuls onto a paper plate, broke off a piece of the French bread he had wrapped carefully in cellophane and went to the chair by the window.

It was a small window that looked out to the street. Across the street was the Hurry and Go. Next to that was the Sav-Time Laundromat. On the other side was Tom's Bicycle Repair. At the corner was the old Avenue Theater that had been closed even before he went to work for Bill, its walls covered by graffiti.

Monkey chewed slowly and watched the street. People were in the laundromat. He could see them shaking out towels, folding shirts. A red neon wheel turned at Tom's Bicycle Repair. In front of the Hurry and Go a black Pontiac Grand Prix, like the one he had worked on just that morning, obscured his view of the poster of a fat man running that stood beside the swinging glass doors.

Monkey did not think about the woman. He did not think about anything particularly. Frank's black-and-white television was on a packing crate against the far wall, but he seldom turned it on. The batteries for the Walkman Bill had given him one Christmas were dead, and he hadn't bought new ones. There were a few magazines about automobiles and motorcycles, which Bill subscribed to for customers to read while they drank instant coffee and waited. Sometimes he read those and thought about vehicles he had worked on. He remembered each one, as a surgeon recalls every operation. So this evening he looked at the black Pontiac parked in front of the Hurry and Go and remembered the car he had repaired that morning.

His mind had found the fuel filter beneath the carburetor, had gotten it free and replaced, when he heard a pop, pop from the street below, a thin, quick sound. Then pop, pop, pop, and the door of the

Hurry and Go flew open. Three young men ran out. Monkey leaned forward. The men came under the street light. He saw their faces, brown young men with black, straight hair. They jumped into the car and sped away. But Monkey's brain, as automatic as the machines he used to test compression and the exhaust of engines, had recorded the license plate of the Grand Prix.

People came out of the laundromat. A woman carried an orange towel. She waved it at the Hurry and Go. A man, whose bald head shone like oil, tucked a pair of socks into his back pocket and stepped to the door of the Hurry and Go. Monkey watched him disappear inside. In a moment the man ran out. He said something to the woman. She clapped the orange towel over her mouth, jumped into the laundromat and slammed the door. The man ran up the street a bit, ran back, and stood fidgeting by the picture of the fat man. Then a black-and-white, its red lights shivering, came up. Two officers got out. They ran into the Hurry and Go with the bald man. Monkey went to the refrigerator and got a bottle of beer.

He opened it and sat at the window drinking. A second police car arrived.

There were more people. He recognized the woman with the orange towel, who wore a sweater now and carried a wicker basket. An officer talked to her, then to some of the others. The officer went to the curb. He looked up and down the street. He looked across the street. Then he saw Monkey by the open window holding a bottle of beer.

The officer crossed the street and stood on the sidewalk in front of the double doors that opened into the garage.

"How long have you been there?" the officer said.

"Since I've been eating," Monkey replied.

"Did you see anything at the Hurry and Go?" the officer said.

"I saw a black Pontiac Grand Prix," Monkey said. "Parked there."

"When was that?" the officer said.

"Not long ago," Monkey said.

"How long?"

"Since before when I sat down to eat."

The officer cocked his head. "I'd like to ask you some more questions, then." He shifted his weight.

"I'll come down there," Monkey said, ducking into the room.

He put the beer into the refrigerator, padlocked the room, went down the stairs into the garage, drew back the bolt on the double doors. He stepped outside. The officer had a notebook in his hands. He was a head taller than Monkey.

"What's your name?" the officer said.

"Monkey," he said.

"Monkey? What's Monkey?"

"Monkey Wertzner."

"What are you doing up there?" the officer asked.

"I live there."

"What did you see?" the officer said.

"I saw a black Pontiac Grand Prix. I heard a popping noise. Pop. Pop. Pop. I saw three men run out of the Hurry and Go. I saw them get into the Grand Prix and drive away."

"What time was this?"

"After I finished work."

"What were you doing?"

"I was eating. I eat right after work."

"Did you see what they looked like?"

"They were dark. With black hair. They were young."

"That's all you saw."

"I saw the license."

The officer pulled him across the street. He opened the door of a police car. When Monkey gave him the number, the officer spoke it into a microphone.

"That was very helpful, Mr. Wertzner," the officer said.

"Monkey," he said. "Nobody says Mr. Wertzner."

"Well, Monkey," the officer said, "with that information we'll get them sure. It's a good thing you were having dinner there."

"I was eating," Monkey said. "That's what I always do after work."

The officer nodded and stepped back.

*   *   *

Monkey went back to his room over the garage. He got the bottle of beer from the refrigerator and the apple, the first half of which he had eaten the night before. He went to the window.

There were more officers. The woman with the laundry basket had gone. The bald man stood to one side. Then a van arrived. A man rolled a long table into the Hurry and Go. He came out with something under a sheet, put it into the van and drove away. A yellow tape was stretched in front of the Hurry and Go.

The officers stayed for awhile. Someone in a dark suit and tie finally put out the lights and locked the glass doors.

People were in the laundromat. The red neon wheel turned at Tom's Bicycle Repair. Monkey saw an object lying at the curb. He went down the stairs, opened the double doors, crossed the street and bent over. It was a pair of socks. He took them upstairs.

The following morning a white station wagon stopped at the garage. Some people got out and went into the office. Monkey had his head under the hood of a 1984 Ford Mustang when Bill tapped him on the shoulder.

"Hey, Monkey. Some folks from Channel 36. They want to talk to you."

"From what?" His face was smudged with grease.

"The television," Bill said. "About last night."

Monkey looked at the people. A boy with long blond hair balanced a camera on one shoulder. A man in a bow tie and plaid coat carried a leather case with silver handles. A young woman with bright blue eyes, who looked like something taken from a shelf, held a wireless microphone.

"You are Mr. Wertzner," the woman declared, in an even voice.

"Monkey," Monkey said.

The woman looked at her friends. "Well, Monkey, I'm Kay Jarret from Channel 36 News. You've seen us."

Monkey looked at Bill, who tapped him on the elbow.

"I don't know," Monkey said.

The woman took a step forward. "Well, Monkey," she said, "we'd like to talk to you some. About last night. You're a hero, you know."

"Hero," Monkey said.

"They caught the men. Didn't you know? The license plate. All three. From the Hill Gang. Haven't you heard?"

He shook his head.

"It was you who caught them, Monkey. You'll be on television. Tonight. Channel 36. What do you think about it?"

Bill clapped him on the back. The other men from the garage, Boyd Nease and Wayne Bolewine, stood nearby, gaping.

Monkey stepped away. "I don't know nothing," he replied.

"It's not what you know," Bill said, as he smiled at the TV woman. "It's what you did. That's it." He looked at the name of the garage stitched on Monkey's shirt. "Maybe he should clean up a little first," he said. "Before he goes on."

"No. Don't do that," the woman said. "This is authentic. A regular citizen. Who did his duty. What our viewers can relate to. Don't you see it? A grease monkey. Michael, are you ready?"

The boy stepped back and put the camera against his face as Bill cleaned the company logo on Monkey's shirt. Monkey took the rag from Bill and rubbed his hands. A bright light snapped on. The woman started to talk. Monkey raised his blackened arms.

Later a Cadillac Seville stopped at Heimer's Garage. Two men in suits went into the office. Monkey was working on a Chevy Caprice. Boyd and Wayne walked to the car and Boyd said, "Hey, something's up again. Why are you getting the breaks?"

Monkey looked at the office door. The men came out. Bill smiled, even more than when Channel 36 was there.

"Hey, Monkey," Bill said. "This is Mr. Henderson and Mr. Schaeffer from the Hurry and Go chain. They have something for you."

"Monkey," Mr. Henderson said, smiling awkwardly when he pronounced the name, "your alertness and courage have brought to justice the evil that struck us across the street last night. We're proud of you. We'd like you to have this little token of our gratitude. What you did will help discourage further brutalization of this neighborhood."

Mr. Henderson handed Monkey a check. Monkey stared at it. Wayne peered over Monkey's shoulder. His lips parted. Boyd raised an eyebrow. Wayne lifted one hand, fingers spread.

"I can't," Monkey said.

"But you must," Mr. Henderson said. "It's a small price."

"I can't use this," said Monkey.

"Take it, Monkey," Bill said. "You deserve it."

"I was eating," Monkey said. "I didn't do nothing. I can't use this."

Mr. Henderson said to his colleague. "Can you beat it, Frank?"

"Refreshing," Mr. Schaeffer replied.

"Then anything you want. Anytime. You just go across to the Hurry and Go, and you ask. That's all there is to it. You hear, Mr. Wertzner? That's all."

"But—" Monkey began.

"Now, now," Mr. Henderson said, touching the only clean spot on Monkey's shoulder, "you're a good man."

That night Bill invited Monkey for dinner and to watch the news on color TV. Monkey spent a half hour scrubbing himself. He patted scented water on his blue shirt and khaki pants. He put on the shoes he kept in a paper bag under the sink.

Bill's sons, Barney and Chris, who played jokes on him when they came to the garage, looked at Monkey and kept silent. Bill's wife, Kim, padded about the table, handing him things. They went into the family room.

Monkey sat in the La-Z-Boy with his feet up. There was a cup of coffee and a second piece of lemon meringue pie on the table beside him.

The woman with blue eyes appeared. She sat behind a desk, a large number 36 over her left shoulder. Monkey watched as she told what had happened. Then there he was, standing with his arms at his sides, holding a rag from the five-gallon pail. When he heard his own voice coming through the TV, he didn't recognize it, and by the time he did, the woman was talking about an automobile accident on the interstate. Bill was now looking at Monkey. Bill's wife and two sons were looking at him. Everyone was smiling.

Then Bill was driving him back to the garage, it seemed such a short time had passed. Monkey went upstairs to his room and stood before the refrigerator. He placed an arm on either side of the picture on the refrigerator door. He removed the blue shirt and looked. He removed the khaki pants and looked at the photograph. He turned his back and looked again, carefully, over his shoulder. Then he got a bottle of beer, went to the window and sat down.

He watched the street and drank the beer. The Hurry and Go was lit up. Inside were the shelves and everything on them. Outside, next to the glass doors, was the poster of the fat man running.

Monkey drank the beer. The street was empty. The laundromat was dark. The wheel over Tom's Bicycle Repair blinked. He finished the beer. After a time he pulled the blanket back on the cot and lay down. He looked at the ceiling. He looked for a long time before he went to sleep.

Early in the morning four young men got into Heimer's Garage and climbed the stairs to Monkey's room. They hit Monkey with a lug wrench and dumped him out of the cot. His head was against the floor. They hit him as he lay on the floor. One of them drew a moustache on the face of the woman and a swastika under each of her small breasts.

When Bill took the police up later, they saw the photograph and shook their heads. Bill talked about how hard it was to really know someone. It didn't matter. By now she was very old, or dead too.

The Beggar of Union Square

He spraddles the sidewalk, hunched against a trash bin, his raggy, striped cat on a dirty sash between his legs. He holds the cardboard sign, which reads, "Sick. No work. Please help. Homeles." The cardboard is so old that it could have been created when cardboard was invented.

I lean against the new Macy's building. Across Geary the grass above the underground parking garage still shines with dew. At the far end of the block, upon a concrete pedestal that leads to the benches and shrubbed plaza above the garage, where a Venezuelan band plays gourds and whistles, sits a young man, frozen in an attitude of placid expectation, painted silver, from hair to shoe, facing the intersection. Occasionally a tourist in Bermuda shorts or cotton skirt drops change into a silver cap. Immediately Metal Man jerks to life, moves stiffly, nods in gratitude, then returns to immobility.

Great buildings rise to meet an ice-blue box of sky where gulls and pigeons turn. Union Square, San Francisco. The West Coast Coliseum of Consumption.

At least Metal Man offers some return for a contribution. The other panhandlers, enough to field a basketball team, are a literary lot, out of Dickens, Hardy, or Crane. Dishevelled, dirty, waxen-eyed, shameless, they hold positions on the sidewalk as if, eight o'clock at the hall, they had been assigned locations and allotted stubby animals, used newspapers, and wrinkled, khaki grocery bags by a kind of slovenly seniority that makes them as much a fixture for the locals, who ignore them, as the rich, leathery things behind polished windows.

My man is the best at getting tourists to buy forgiveness. He offers it with blazing, blood-streaked eyes, pale, drawn face, nails cracked and undercut by some dark, oily substance he constantly picks at in ritualistic deference to cleanliness, instinctive, like the pink tongue of the raggy cat who sits between his legs and seeks to rid its fur of the odor and exhaust of the street. A master at making each person who passes and holds his gaze long enough feel the sunlight of that morning's water and soap, he nudges his cap gently, encouraging them to scrub, with a few coins, that tiny filth that has been missed and to wash it down the drain of his despair.

Living on Diamond Heights above the city, shrouded in fog, tempered by damp air that blows in from the sea, solaced by the view of an empty, wooded canyon down which hawks still fly, I have made my attempt at reconciliation. Yet, either from the requisites of business or a need, at times, to affirm some vanity about life, I travel downtown and linger among strangers who have come from around the world to buy.

He is always for sale, the final "s" gone from his advertisement. No one else has made this error. In the politics of San Francisco every citizen knows the grammar. It is printed in newspapers, taped to traffic lights and bulletin boards, displayed on trolley cars that rumble to Fisherman's Wharf and commuter trains that slide beneath the bay to Lafayette and Walnut Creek. Tambourines, horns, and drums chant its alphabet in bench-lined rooms of crusty men. The whisper of silk and flannel makes a proper spelling along the cushioned seats of Davies Hall. It is as though, reduced to the level of the street, below which there can be no lower place, he has yet found an absolute degradation: his final "s" is homeless too.

He is a master. He never speaks, neither smiles nor pouts. He hardly moves, except to offer meaty scraps, which he keeps in a cellophane bag inside his coat, to the stripy cat, whose tongue is hypnotic in its futility, or to nudge the cap with bony fingertips. His eyes hunt the approaching flock. In his slumped, broken tenure with the concrete, from which he is separated only by a tattered scrap of burlap, he cups his head.

Bloodshot eyes roll, fixing themselves like leeches. Quarters and dimes drop, in stooped bombing runs of mercy and guilt. Sometimes even a green bill or two finds its way, laid carefully, usually by women, across the opening of his filthy cap. I have never seen him touch this paper money, but always, if I glance away just for a moment, attracted by Metal Man or a flamboyance from Miami, the bills have gone. No one, after all, must understand that generosity might raise him above the need to beg. He recognizes me and knows I have been watching.

I make my decision.

He will be on duty until four. There is plenty of time. If I return to Diamond Heights, I will get comfortable and won't return. So I wander up the street to O'Doul's for corned beef, a beer and a little conversation with the bartender, who keeps two television sets on above the rows of bottles. It is pleasant to sit there just inside the door and watch golf or baseball or the people on the street.

At three-thirty precisely I return to Union Square, proceed past Metal Man, who does not move a mechanical lash, and take up a position in the plaza which allows me to peer down through the shrubs without being seen.

He is there, slumped against the trash bin, his head bowed a bit, the cat asleep, finally, in the shadow of the street sign. Even from here I can see that only a few coins lie in the dirty cap beneath the cardboard sign, which he has braced to his chest. Exhausted, pitiable and clever, he knows it is near quitting time and is taking a breather. The current of tourists, now that he does not look, streams by, faces washed by the odd, afternoon light that plays off the buildings, relieved by the indifference he seems to display regarding his condition. And why shouldn't he relax? The pocket of his grimy coat is bulging.

At four o'clock he rises, gathers the cat, which, I am convinced, has been drugged to docility, under his arm, folds the sign carefully, then hurries off along the street, disappearing around the Macy's building down Stockton toward Market. I run across the patch of lawn, jump to the sidewalk, and make the corner just in time to see him cross O'Farrell, the head of the cat bumping above his shoulder. At Market he turns left, and by the time I draw up, just close enough so that, if he turns back, I can duck away, he has skipped across Grant and gone into the gray, pillared Wells Fargo Building.

Stunned, but not enough to lose that sense of irony which, in this city, allows one to survive, I quietly push open the door and glide to an ATM machine, where I can observe and appear busy at the same time.

No one seems to mind the stripy cat or the grime as my man empties his pocket and builds a mound of crumpled bills upon the counter before the thick, bulletproof window. He is only another businessman making deposits at the end of a profitable day. When he is done, receipt in hand and head held at a jaunty angle, he strides out the door into the afternoon light.

He is not so old as I once thought. I put him at around thirty-five.

Staying a few yards behind, I follow him up Grant, the cat still comfortably drugged and indifferent. He enters Chinatown and vanishes into a stairwell between two shops. There are apartments above some of these buildings. I purchase a small bag of sugared fruit, light a corona and, because his urgency intrigues me even more, decide to wait. Halfway through the cigar, I see him emerge from the stairwell freshly scrubbed, wearing a blue blazer, gray gabardine slacks, a white polo shirt, and tasseled, newly polished, cordovan loafers. He strides to the corner of Grant and Bush and hails a cab, which whisks him away toward Van Ness.

The sonofabitch.

It takes me five days to produce enough beard. In the meantime I employ an old scouring pad to grind dirt and 3-in-One Oil into old sneakers I've found at the back of a closet. I fray a worn pair of tan cotton pants, a gray work shirt, a poplin jacket, and a tweed cap I bought in Dublin many years before. I grind all of these things against the pavement of the covered garage beneath my building, using every spot of damp grit I can find. By Saturday, in the height of the tourist season, I am ready.

That morning, well before the shops have opened or Metal Man has given the final luster to his silver skin or the other panhandlers have taken their assigned posts along the streets, I have sprawled upon the sidewalk before Macy's, my back against the trash bin. I have no battered dog or cat, since I will not assume that kind of responsibility, but I do have my scrap of burlap, my billed, filthy cap open between my legs and my square of cardboard, which I have bent so many times that it looks like something placed long ago at the bottom of a garbage can. It reads: "Help. Please. Sick. No work. Homeles."

I collect $15.85 from early, peripatetic tourists before the shops open, Metal Man occupies his position at the corner of Geary and Powell, or my man arrives, animal tucked, sign unfolded, striding comfortably down Stockton Street from Chinatown. When he sees me, he almost drops the cat.

I, of course, pretend not to notice. Head bowed above my mealy sign, down and out, ashamed, humiliated, reduced, beneath pride, to the street, I am new here and know nothing of vagrant, union-shop perks or beggarly primogeniture. I am trying to save my life.

"Hey!" a voice snaps.

I move my head as if wounded, squinting as though recovering from a drunken stupor the night before.

"Hey," the voice comes again, a bit softer. "That's my spot, you know. You've taken my spot, man."

I do not understand. I try to watch him out of the swirl in my brain. I am Quasimodo upon the rack, pleading for water. I am Gianni Schicchi.

"My spot," he says, haltingly.

I drop my head, push my sign forward, tap my cap brokenly. Speech, certainly, implies some milk of human kindness. I look up, my eyes clouded, my face carefully grimed, my hair clotted by grease and soil, groomed from the flower bed outside my window.

"Please. Help," I whisper.

He is astounded. I have not seen his rags, not noticed his scabrous sign, his own tattered scrap of burlap, which he clutches so tightly against the drugged animal that the cat, even in its stupor, unsheathes its claws and buries them into his shoulder.

He takes a step back, confronted by the anomaly of himself, anxious that something real may have found its way into his theater of the absurd. My heart laughs. I have won the audition, with as much talent as I display in my office above the Embarcadero. I twitch the cap a bit more.

"Please," I whisper. "In God's name."

He hesitates, looking up and down the sidewalk, as though a shop steward might appear to settle his claim. We must be a sight, brothers of the street, companions of the underpass, sharers of the soup kitchen and the tax write-offs of Nob Hill. Even here, at the bottom, there is competition, a notion he never conceived of.

A moment more and he stumbles away, clutching his cat. I remain until quitting time.

And that should have been the end of it.

That night I stay under the shower for thirty minutes trying to wash away what I have done. But there is no remorse. I have outphonied the Prince of Phonies. My humiliation and despair have met his, have triumphed. My lost "s" is more abandoned than his own.

Standing before the mirror later, I am amazed at the minimalist quality of my achievement. With determination anyone might have done it. The trick, I discovered almost immediately, was in not being there, since people don't care who you are and regard your dismal, obscure suffering as a mask behind which to hide, with some loose change, their own indifference. The real man is the one who makes the deposit in the bank after a day's work, climbs the steps to a furnished apartment in Chinatown, spruces up, and, attired from a sale at Brooks Brothers, catches a cab to North Beach.

And so, when I dress, gather up the eighty-odd dollars I have earned, drive to a church in the Tenderloin and drop it all into the poor box, I feel a warmth and nobleness of purpose I have not known for some time. The poor have gotten the money after all. Isn't that what the tourists expected? I have done, then, a good deed. No one has been cheated, except The Beggar of Union Square.

But I keep the scruffy beginning of my beard and, the following morning, take it to the office above the Embarcadero.

There is a lot of good-natured kidding about lost youth, gold chains, silk shirts, red Targas, gambling trips with painted women to Lake Tahoe. Tiffany Adams, who works in the office next to mine, suggests that I pare it to a moustache. A moustache, she insists, looks sexy, less seedy. Bart Hofstadler, who owns the company, says he once tried to grow a beard on a fishing vacation to Montana, but it annoyed him later under stiff, white collars and bow ties. He frowns, smiling, because he knows how indispensable I am, and says, "It's up to you."

I understand it is and say so, happily. I have never let any of them in, maintaining a privacy that borders almost upon anonymity. I hate the thought of gossip and minding one another's business. They know of the failed marriages and the children who have gone away. They have validated my silences in bars and lounges along Broadway. I am not someone they would have home to dinner.

That night I lay out my beggar's rags upon the floor, uncertain what it is that I have proved. My man's performance has been disrupted for a day. My colleagues have found more reason to doubt my sociability. Really, nothing is changed.

The jacket, pants, shoes, and shirt, though filthy, are like those old, threadbare things I found in my mother's closet when she died, my father's clothes that she kept hanging next to her blouses and dresses after he had gone. The cap I bought in Ireland reminds me of the one he wore to the games at Kezar.

The next morning, Saturday, I sit behind the shrubs above the garage at Union Square to watch my man beg. I do not want him to see me now, since I have decided to keep, for a time, my new beard. He has dismissed my intrusion, I am sure, as an aberration in the business of the street. His sign is out. His raggy cat licks itself continuously. He begs, with a quiet ferocity, the parade of tourists up and down Geary. His tattered coat pocket begins to fill. Periodically he jingles the cap, lifting the cardboard slowly, as though it were lead. It is a perfect, limited performance, practiced so often that his brain, I am sure, is in Chinatown watching television or dreaming about what awaits him that night at North Beach.

After all, what harm is done? He is providing a service, releasing each contributor from just enough guilt to maintain a useful life.

Yet, the following morning, bright and early, in costume, grimed and greased, I am at his station again, my sign tucked beneath my chin, a torn, wrinkled lunch bag—my own extrapolation of poverty—spread open upon the sidewalk between my legs. My cap I clutch tightly against my chest, as though I have just wrung it from my head in a desperate, final gesture of prayer and hopelessness, in that masterstroke of method acting which I realized, even days before, as a contribution I might make to this drama of the street. In the hour before he arrives, I have collected $25.30.

I spot him from beneath lowered head and narrowed eyes. He stands just out of the intersection of Geary and Stockton, his ugly cat across his shoulder, his cardboard sign limp at his side. Mouth agape, dumbfounded, he can come no further. I repress a desire to smile and instead shake the coins into a tiny pile in the center of my paper sack.

He watches as, without so much as a glance, I convince pilgrims from Syracuse and St. Paul to find it within their hearts to help a fellow down on his luck. I beat my cap against my breast in a mea culpa of regret. I absolve them of everything. It is a brilliant show, so much so that even he, standing impotent at the threshold to his concrete office, shakes his head slowly in disbelief that something genuine has taken his place.

A few minutes more and he turns quickly on his heel and heads toward Chinatown.

That night all that I have collected—over one hundred dollars—rests before me upon the kitchen table. I am repelled. I am frightened. I wish there were a way without asking for money. I bundle it up to take to a mission at Hunters Point. On the way down I realize that there is something as unobtainable here as a fast ride home over the Bay Bridge at rush hour, and that I live, shut in at the top of the city, only to escape the abuse of traffic.

Early the next morning I leave a message on the machine at work saying that I will be ill for a time, get made up, and head to the sidewalk at Macy's.

I turn my sign around.

The people are as objects in a current, and I am a rock around which they must flow. My hat pulled close about my eyes—for I am so embarrassed now that I can barely raise my head—I lift one hand, palm up, and reveal the unspeakable, the simple, urgent syllable which I have scribbled on the other side of my cardboard: "Love."

I am met with looks as peculiar and as distant as if I had been discovered crushed beneath the wheels of a taxi in the street. It is a terrible thing, an awful thing, but, as the morning wears on, and I believe that no one I see can possibly recognize me, I energize my performance, lifting one arm, then the other, sometimes both, pushing myself up from my scrap of burlap as though I would fasten upon them should they bend too near. I roll my eyes. I wet my lips. The faces from Syracuse and St. Paul are shocked. I am loose from a private room on the other side of town, an idiot gotten free among the sane. By noon I reach a pitch so feverish and obscure that people gather to stare, as they do for Metal Man. I fear the police may come, but I am beside myself. At the end, without a penny to show for my effort, exhausted at last, I sweep my cap to my breast, lower my head, turn the sign around and, as the money rolls in, find some sense of the separation my beggar must feel as, clean and coiffed, he saunters out of his apartment for a night on the town.

That evening I count my take, a much smaller amount, of course, since I have lost the entire morning, drive to the mission, return home, collapse into bed and, reliving the morning's performance and longing for the night to be through, fall into a dreamless sleep.

The next day there are no qualms. My mask is complete. I rise to a crescendo of applause, which I find in their blinking, wide eyes and open, toothless mouths. My sign speaks what I cannot say; their pecuniary silence, an offering they cannot make. The luxury of their anonymity, behind the tender mercies of loose change, is at risk. It is a perfect standoff.

I test them and myself throughout the day, flipping the sign first one way, then the other. When I am sick, without work, and "homeles," the cap fills. When I show my word, I am as strange as a sky without color.

That night I put my winnings into a glass bowl and set it upon the table.

The following morning, cap in hand, I have my sign as it should be. The tourists strafe me with the residue of pleasure they have found for a vacation well spent, among shops, restaurants, and weather, in one of the world's most beautiful cities. The coins chink against each other on my paper plate.

I will not show the word again, and though I have beaten my beggar at his game, I wonder what I have won.

The hours go. The peace of pretending, seated at the bottom of the square, inured to traffic and the press of people, gives new meaning to solitude and loneliness. The secret is not to take life seriously, to feed the cat, get dressed, and head for a good time at North Beach.

Suddenly he is there, the blue blazer buttoned across gray gabardine slacks, the tasseled loafers shining, a red-and-blue power tie perfectly centered against a white, button-down shirt. He points one clean, manicured finger and screams, "Fake!"

I gape at him, my cardboard pressed against my chest, my feeble pile of coins gleaming dully before me.

"A fake!" the beggar screams again. "I followed him home yesterday! He lives in a fancy apartment on Diamond Heights!"

The people stop. They look at me and then at my accuser.

"I'm telling you!" the beggar shouts. "I followed him! He's not homeless! He lives on Diamond Heights! He's a fake!"

My filth, the grime of my costume, my raggy scrap of burlap, my cardboard sign, my beard keep me safe, but I feel as if I am seen for the first time, exactly as I came into this world. The sight of him, arms crossed in triumphant revenge, smirking, and my own tattered mortification, the irony of which no one of the tourists from Syracuse or Miami can possibly comprehend, leaves me amused and horrified. What can I possibly say? He's telling the truth.

I begin to laugh. I get to my feet, still laughing. I throw down my cap and cardboard sign. I leave the day's take upon the scrap of paper. I walk off toward O'Doul's laughing so hard that, by the time I get to Powell, my eyes are full of tears.

The next morning, cleaned, shaved, and sporting a new suit from Bullock and Jones, I stop a moment at my beggar's stand on the way to work, and, when he lifts his eyes in that practiced, shopworn plea for mercy, drop a crisp, one hundred-dollar bill into his miserly cap.

The Electric Dog

Jonathan McCrorey blew the ash from his cigar and passed out. When he awoke, Midge, the striped mongrel cat who had been abandoned along his country road two years before, lay on the concrete pad six inches from his face, staring expectantly. With some difficulty he pushed himself to a sitting position. The cat crawled into his lap and dug its nails into his thigh. "What the hell's going on here?" he demanded of the roses he had been pruning, and went cautiously to the kitchen pantry for the Kit 'n Kaboodle.

The cat ate greedily, purring, hunched above the purple dish in a posture timeless to feeding things. He watched for a while. A line of beaded sweat formed across his brow.

Marian was upstate visiting her mother, a crotchety old stump who believed that space creatures had once landed in the fields near Roswell, New Mexico. He believed in aliens himself, but only as a matter of logic. They must exist somewhere, he reasoned, beyond any star touched by the Hubble telescope, a kind of necessary postulate in the formulations of science, which had found, thus far, only limitless space and the absence of God.

It was just as well. He was uncomfortable telling Marian about what went on inside. She was prone to hysteria. She had grown this way more so of late, worried about thieves, murderers, and rapists at an exponential rate commensurate with the evening news. She had even made him purchase Max, The Electric Dog, which she had seen advertised in a mail-order catalog that had come to the house addressed to "occupant," as though any human anywhere must see the necessity, these days, of positioning such an instrument so that, at a moment's notice, it might signal any movement in the darkness beyond. Max sounded remarkably real and barked once at the first movement, several times for the next, and then in a rising crescendo of threatening growls for every movement thereafter. They had tested Max, who could detect motion through walls, and though Midge, scrambling along the windowsill, might set him off, or a stray bird or even a brisk wind swaying the potted bamboo, so that, more than once, Marian had sat upright in bed, pushing him awake to open the sliding closet door and fumble for the shotgun, it was, she argued, the only way she could sleep in the summer with the windows of the house rolled open. He tolerated it, of course, for harmony's sake, but after a time, even when she was away visiting, he set the dog out before retiring. Subconsciously, he supposed, he had become inured to Max's electric vigilance.

That night he watched a special on PBS about the Pathfinder. For months the device had hurtled through space guided by signals from Earth, to arrive safely at last upon the surface of Mars, bouncing to a stop in something that resembled a grotesque beach ball. Out of the ball had crawled Rover, a mechanical beast the size of a Pomeranian. It sniffed rocks, transmitted amazing pictures millions of miles to his living room, where he sat alone, eating chocolate graham crackers and sipping milk he had warmed in the microwave. Already Rover had discovered that an immense flood had once covered the Martian plain. There would be enough information, scientists said, to occupy them for years.

When the program was done, he shut off the set, placed Max upon the piano bench facing the west windows, and went into the bathroom. He was not particularly tired and did not want to lie down, yet he knew that if he stayed up, he would pay for it in the morning. Even as a boy, he had needed a good eight hours each night. He lay awake until twelve before surrendering to sleep.

At two o'clock something moved in the jasmine outside the living room windows, but Max did not bark. A drunken teenager had killed himself moments before against a power pole on Davis Road. Jonathan McCrorey, turning restlessly in bed, sat up.

He understood, of course, that the power was off. The light on the clock was out, as was the switch on the wall, which always glowed a pale, incandescent orange. He picked up the flashlight he kept on the nightstand and walked down the hall into the kitchen. He opened and closed the refrigerator door, then called Pacific Gas and Electric. A recorded message told him the problem was being attended to.

He went into the living room and sat down in the dark. There was a thump against the house. He stood, pulled back the curtains, tried to shine the light through the window, but saw nothing. A half hour later the power came back, Max barked, then growled when he stood up. He smiled and returned to bed.

The next morning he sat at the kitchen table drinking coffee and watching the *Today Show*. There was more about Mars. They were giving names to the rocks Rover touched, silly names, to his way of thinking, for something so vastly significant from so far away. Rover's treaded feet scratched forward an inch at a time. His tiny sensors clawed up data only computers could understand. Somewhere beyond the year 2000, they said, men would walk where Rover had gone. He was so hypnotized by the marvel of it all that when a commercial about detergent appeared, he became angry.

He had never passed out before.

The heat of that afternoon, the fact that he had walked eighteen holes without a hat, that he hadn't taken in water, that he had come home and then immediately gone out to the roses were sufficient explanations, when he thought about it that evening. He had done such things more than once before, with no ill effect, yet, memory does eclipse, he considered, and, the power returned, and Max once more on duty, he understood that time had passed, that he was no longer a young man, that he should always use sunblock and perhaps ride a cart across the 7,200 yard country club course. Marian's increased admonitions about health and diet, her nervousness about what might occur in the yard after dark should be seen in that light.

But this morning, alone in the kitchen, sipping yesterday's coffee, thrilled by a tiny mechanical creature that had traveled so far to learn, gently, of a desolate world, he was aware of something more, something serrated about the beating of his heart. He switched off the television and listened. He put a hand to his chest. He sat quite still. There were, indeed, odd ridges and valleys. A bead of sweat broke out across his forehead.

He went immediately to Dr. Frank, whose office was on the seventh floor of the old Medical-Dental Building downtown. He did not like going to doctors, which, of course, was irrational, for he was astonished, as well, by the developments in medical research. Transplanted organs. The cloning of sheep. A Rand McNally atlas of the human gene. People frozen beyond any earthly cold in steel wombs waiting for final discoveries which would allow them to be born again into everlasting life.

A few moments of unexplained sleep while pruning roses would be as nothing in the face of such achievement.

Dr. Frank, a short, fat man with the smell of cigarettes upon his breath, listened good-naturedly to his description of what had happened. The doctor put a stethoscope against his chest, against his back between his shoulders, moved it to one side of his neck, then the other.

"Aha," the doctor said. "We must do some tests."

"Shall I make an appointment, then?" Jonathan McCrorey asked.

"Now," the doctor said evenly.

He was sent to an office on the third floor where, wires attached, he strode upon a rolling black mat that rose steadily before him until, his heart thudding upon deeper ruts, his eyes filled with sweat, he could no longer continue, and stepped away, just under four minutes. He was dizzy and had to sit down.

That evening, with Marian returned, cowering alone in the waiting room and absolutely no consolation, he was engineered to sleep and then entered, near the groin, by a miniature lens that crept up his body to take pictures of his heart.

When he awoke and was comfortable, the doctor explained that there was some blockage in one of the arteries, which hadn't been expected yet could be easily repaired, but, as he had surmised earlier, the nature of the heart itself had been the source of the sudden swoon near the roses.

"What do you mean by that?" Jonathan McCrorey asked, his eyes wide.

The doctor had brought along a flesh-tinted plastic heart, which opened in the center to expose an array of finely painted surfaces and tubes. He explained that the heart was a machine, like any other, and required fuel, which was obtained from lines running into it, that it functioned, faster or slower, according to the demands upon it, and that its rhythm should be regularly proportionate to those demands.

The doctor put the heart together, opening and closing his free hand like the swing of a pendulum.

"Sometimes, though," the doctor said, "with age, the heart stumbles." His hand jerked open, clamped shut. "It misfires, as it were. The timing gets off. We have to go in and," he smiled, "—well, tune it up."

Marian, who had come in to sit stiffly beside the bed, now leaned forward. She had not blinked since Dr. Frank entered the room.

"An operation, you mean," Jonathan McCrorey said.

"A simple thing," the doctor said. "Done thousands of times. Like going to a garage for a minor service." He smiled broadly.

"What—what will you do?" Marian asked tremulously.

"Lift up a flap of skin just here," the doctor replied, touching his chest, "install a mechanism to regulate the beat, then sew it shut. And you're home in a day or two. That's it."

"A pacemaker," Marian said.

"A pacemaker," the doctor repeated, smiling.

"Jonathan," Marian said, "Ted Diamond has a pacemaker."

"You'll do everything you did before," the doctor said, "and more."

"Ted plays tennis, now, three times a week," Marian said, enthusiastic.

"A pacemaker," Jonathan McCrorey said.

"That's it," the doctor said.

He closed his eyes a moment, trying to imagine himself walking, eating, showering, making love, while a toy robot regulated his heart.

"But how does it work?" he asked. "What makes it go?"

"Batteries," the doctor said. "Miniature, high-powered batteries. On the order of this." He tapped his watch. "You won't know it's there."

Two days after the operation Jonathan McCrorey was home. Marian had stayed in a hotel, not wanting to be alone in the house at night. He understood, of course, but was annoyed. She hovered over him, encouraging rest, but he was strangely elated and went out to the roses. They needed water, naturally. The whole yard needed water. He walked about, turning valves, moving hoses. He felt giddy, light-headed. But it was fine. It was as though his brain had filled with oxygen, and there wasn't enough to do. He could hardly wait to be out at the club, and swung his arms slowly above the living room rug in anticipation.

Marian prepared special dishes, which, at first, he declined to eat. He had a ravenous appetite for pork and beef and sometimes slipped off to the fast-food on the outskirts of town when she was shopping. He experienced euphoria, accompanied by renewed vigor, which, at last, permitted him to stride bareheaded from shot to shot on the golf course, and scissor the roses, shrubs, and jasmine with unexpected joy.

She became absolutely concerned for his health, pecking about him like a nesting hen. She bought recipe books, books about diet, books about exercise. She obtained special directions from the doctor, regimens from clinics, fastening them to the refrigerator door. She bought a scale, measured everything carefully, made notes in a spiral-bound book. Without all this attention, this care, these special directions, now, about how to live, he must surely harm himself. The body was an instrument, naturally designed, which must be kept constantly in adjustment if it was to operate properly. Finally, he agreed. He had been careless, and then lucky. After the initial glee of renewed energy had settled, he came to want this more than she did. "Certainly, dear," she whispered one night after they had made more than common love and just before he drifted off to sleep, "I'm thinking only of you." For which he was glad, more so than he had thought possible, even though, about two o'clock that morning, he came awake to find her sitting straight up in bed, watching him.

The news from Mars had flickered out. Television was that way. He recalled the first journey into space. All the channels had carried it. People couldn't get enough of men hitting golf balls on the moon. Now the shuttle went up and back behind drive-by shootings, child molestations, vandalism and forty-point dips in the Dow. The growth of human intelligence, which reached now to stand upon the stars themselves, had been relegated to thirty-second sound-bites after the miseries of Hollywood divorce and hurricanes off the Florida coast. The knowledge that had sent rockets past the sun reached now into his own heart, guiding all with meticulous grace. The uniformity and consistency were never so amazing as when he crouched upon the first tee at the club, adjusted to a more abundant health, and for a moment gazed up at the sky, far beyond whose blue, shimmering veil, miniature extensions of the human mind tiptoed across an alien world. Was not the earth itself a ship navigating through space, bound by laws of celestial mechanics, and all its people simple passengers upon a magnificent voyage? While his imagination soared, those others—and they seemed legion—were content to watch soap operas and reruns of *Roseanne.* He could not fathom such indifference. Even Marian, hovering about him with eggbeaters and one-percent milk, was enervated by the VCR. The human race, he concluded, was a vegetable before its own uniqueness.

One afternoon weeks later Marian came home from the market and set the packages upon the kitchen table, where he was making tea. Her hands were trembling.

"What is it?" he said. "What's wrong?"

"Jonathan," she squeaked, "I met Doris McKenzie, from over on Shelby Road, in the meat department."

"All right," he said, striding into the den to check the news on the public channel.

"Will you please stand still, then," she said.

He stopped, facing her.

"What happened?" he asked languidly.

"Someone broke into their house last night and stole everything."

He put down the cup of tea.

"Where were Doris and Cliff?"

"In bed," she stammered, "sleeping. Oh, Jonathan."

He thought a moment, picturing it in his mind. Cliff was a heavy drinker. Doris had been married two times before.

"We have Max," he said.

"Jonathan, I'm terrified."

"The dog will bark, scare anyone off."

"Jonathan, I absolutely can't sleep now with the windows open."

"We can't sleep with them closed."

"We could shut the ones in the living room, dining room, and laundry room."

"Circulation," he declared. "No circulation. Cliff doesn't lock his doors."

"How do you know they didn't go in through a window?"

"Why would you go in through a window if you could walk in through an unlocked door?"

"Oh, Jonathan, you're impossible," she said. "I'm terrified. Can't you see that? Once they start, they take everyone."

"You don't know that," he insisted.

"Wouldn't you," she said, "when it's so easy?"

"We have the dog," he said. "That's why we bought it. Congratulate yourself and use your head."

"Is the shotgun truly loaded?"

"Of course it's loaded. And we have alarm stickers pasted on the windows."

"Are they going to be reading alarm stickers at three o'clock in the morning? Honestly, Jonathan. Maybe they don't speak English. Have you thought of that?"

"And maybe they're creatures from Roswell, and nothing we can do will stop them anyway. Have you thought of that?"

"Jonathan," she huffed, turning her back, "that's not funny at all."

That night, somewhere after one, there was a thud against the side of the house. Marian, conspicuously, did not stir, but he came awake, in wonder that the device in his chest had perhaps heightened even the level of his subconscious beyond that of Max, who had not made a sound. Flashlight in hand, he crept down the hallway and into the kitchen. He unplugged Max, pulled the dining room curtains, and snapped on the light. Beyond the glare against the glass, he saw nothing, replaced the plug and returned quietly to sleep.

The next morning he found one very large boot print in the soft loam beneath the bedroom window.

Of course, he did not tell Marian. He employed a gardening service from time to time. They had been out the Tuesday before, something as simple as that. It would explain, certainly, why Max had given no warning, since the dog was not on during the day.

He began to take long walks along his country road, in addition to the rounds on the golf course. He lost weight. Each morning for breakfast he ate a grapefruit and cut up a banana on his dry cereal. With fruit juice he swallowed one aspirin and softgels of vitamin C and E. He cut out sodium, substituted fat-free cheese, and drank a glass of red wine with dinner, which consisted, usually, of tossed salad, light Caesar dressing, slices of turkey or chicken breast, and a piece or two of sourdough French bread, to which he applied no butter. He gave up cigars. He had not felt so alive in years.

Marian fluttered about, measuring, writing in the notebook. He was amused by the careful meals she planned, posting them, like grand announcements, upon the refrigerator door. But he was grateful. Without her diligence and support, he might have grown lazy or complacent. They began to talk about a long ocean cruise through the Greek Isles the following summer.

There was still news about the Mars Rover, interspersed between elaborate analyses of serial killing, Muslim militancy in Algeria, and the sexual abuse of children by clerics. He came to suspect that this disproportion between the base, melodramatic, and ugly and the truly glorious and spontaneous in the human struggle, this indifference to the noble and delight in the ignoble, sheltered a failure in the social experiment. How else could one explain the disparity between millions of dollars for those who dribbled basketballs and meager pensions for those who solved quadratic equations? The populism of the commonplace was a denial of genius. Television was a window into the moral shallowness of humanity.

A week later Marian, agitated beyond anything he had yet experienced, returned home to tell him that the Miller house, just up the road, had been entered and that Wayne Miller had been stabbed.

"What!" he declared, sitting down.

"Stabbed," she said, "twice. With a knife from the kitchen cabinet. I told you. I told you. Whatever are we going to do?"

"What about the police?" he asked.

"The police can't be everywhere. Jonathan, I'm terrified. I want to move back to town."

"It's worse there," he said. "That's why we moved to the country, remember?"

"But it's here now too. What are we going to do?"

"All right," he said, "all right. We'll close all the windows at night except those in our bedroom. We can put the little fan on the floor for circulation. How's that?"

She began to cry. He called the sheriff, who reassured him, after he spoke of the precautions he had taken, that there was nothing more he could do, that there were leads, and that, in time, they would certainly apprehend the criminals.

"In the meantime, Mr. McCrorey," the sheriff said finally, "you might leave a light on outside when you go to bed."

That evening it was on television. The reporter stood a quarter of a mile away in the middle of the road. The camera panned up and down. There were the cornfields to the south, Joe Ortega's almond orchard to the west. The reporter philosophized about violence, quoted statistics, then introduced an interview with a university professor, who spoke of economics and the root causes of poverty. He found himself becoming quite angry. The very evil he had sought so assiduously to avoid was here, disguised as information, in his own living room. Forced to endure everything that passed as news for those bits of revelation about the heights of human endeavor, he realized that there was no difference between entertainment and events of the day, nothing that was uplifting or honorable. He demeaned himself, in other words, by watching. The device itself presented everything in uniform, rectangular vulgarity, a failure of human intelligence. He resolved never again to permit himself to be hooked by its insidious appeal. Just at the end of the half hour, almost as an afterthought, there was a mention of Mars, only enough to say that at some time soon the planet would tilt, solar energy would cease, and most would say, finally, of Rover: "Mission accomplished."

That night they closed all the windows in the front part of the house and crawled into bed. The light that had been left on outside bothered him, painting a soft patina of pale yellow upon the curtains. The gentle, even whir of the tiny fan bothered him. The ruffled curl of air across his neck and ears bothered him. Must all summer nights be like this now because of the threat of violence which had entered his life?

He listened to his heart. It was beating faster than he wanted. He was tense and angry, felt helpless and betrayed. Marian moved fitfully into sleep. He could only lie there, alone within himself, frightened by a nameless dread that became, quite gradually, more than any stranger who could not speak English lurking outside or weird-headed aliens from the hayfields around Roswell, New Mexico.

His heart raced, the machine inside his chest pattering out the beats with alarming precision. He tried desperately to be still but could not and drew his legs up to his chest, staring into the yellowed dark.

Suddenly Max barked. Marian sat erect and cried, "Jonathan! Jonathan!"

He moaned oddly, turning from side to side.

"The dog," she said. "The dog. Jonathan!"

She pushed at him like a pillow case stuffed with dirty clothes.

"What's wrong with you?" she pleaded.

Horrified and angry, she crawled over him and stood at the side of the bed. She punched at him.

"Jonathan!"

He rolled over and faced the wall.

Frightened and annoyed, she removed the shotgun from the closet and, clutching the barrel in both hands, crept slowly down the hallway.

High above, on a stone-strewn plain, inhabited only by remnants from a deflated ball, a thing called Rover inched inevitably to rest beneath the arid Martian cold, while below, upon a world grown equally bleak, the electric dog continued to bark, until Marian, reaching the living room at last and discovering that the thing had merely gone off and, through some flaw deep in its nature, had been unable to stop and there was, after all, nothing to fear, pulled the plug.

The Suicide

We all went down to the river to watch Jimmy drown.

He had been talking about it for a long time.

"I'll do it," he said, "you'll see."

"Sure, Jimmy," we told him.

"I will. I'll do it."

"You can't do it," Burr Collins said. "You're a Catholic and Catholics can't drown themselves."

"Who cares?" said Jimmy.

Such disdain for the fires of perdition amazed even us, who had mutually given up all concern for an afterlife the summer before. When you are twelve, the impetus of hedonism is strong, life rests in the shining pages of *Playboy*, suffering seems avoidable, and death is as strange as old Willie Barlow, who lived alone in a shack at the edge of town.

We were friends, Jimmy, Gary, Wilbur (whom we called Burr), and I, and had been since the first grade. It was the kind of friendship made of small town life, where the country backs up to your door, and the world ends where the sun goes down beyond the hills. We had been in the same classes in school, had had the same diseases, had even

127

seen our first naked girl together, that time when we followed the Pontiac up the dirt road along the irrigation canal and peeked over the bank at the emerald green water and the couple skinny-dipping below.

The Mokelumne wasn't a river, really, more like a stream, and we had fished it for trout many times and gone swimming, too, and it wasn't deep, except for Solomon's Pool, named after a man who had landed a seven-pound rainbow there before we were born. Other pools might do the job, but they were a fair hike downstream. Solomon's Pool was just where the Mokelumne crossed under the Southern Pacific Railroad bridge.

"The current's too much anyway," Gary said. "You'd be sucked right into the riffle, and the riffle's only a foot and a half deep."

Gary Stockman's father was weighmaster for the Grange, and Gary always talked like that whenever it was a problem of this or the other. If it was something to figure out, even pulling a nail out of his own foot, Gary was a machine. No feeling. Just something to figure out.

It was summer, and we were almost young, and across the river the poppies were in bloom. There were oak trees along the river and willows too, and further on down wild berry bushes grew to the water's edge. It was a fine place to hunt, and in the autumn we brought our twenty-two's and plinked squirrels that came out of the trees to store nuts for the winter.

"I could hold my breath and dive to the bottom," Jimmy said.

"Nope," said Gary. "Current's too much. You couldn't stay down long enough. You'll just have to find some other way."

We all looked at him, amazed.

"Goddamnit, there isn't any other way," Jimmy said. "That's the way." And he pointed at Solomon's Pool. "I'll figure something out. You'll see."

Except for Gary, I think we were all genuinely frightened at the possibility of "some other way." There were plenty of other ways, of course, we knew that, but they all seemed permanent and incomprehensible. We had been swimming here since we were six. There was nothing scary about Solomon's Pool. So Jimmy, Burr, and I looked at the ground, but Gary only scratched his head.

"Why don't we go over to Burr's and play *Wagon Train?*" I suggested.

Burr's father was a rancher and owned a roan mare and a palomino that were gentle and easy to ride.

"We did that yesterday," Jimmy said.

"Why don't we go throw rocks at Mr. Turturici's house?" Burr said. Mr. Turturici taught English at the high school, and everyone said he was queer.

"We almost got caught that other time," I said.

"But we didn't get caught, did we?" Burr argued.

"It's old," said Jimmy.

"Yeah, old," Gary said.

"Screw you guys, then, you're old," Burr declared. It was always okay to vote no, but it wasn't cool to cap on someone's contribution to the general search for devilment and fun.

"Screw you too," Jimmy said.

"Don't you wish, hermaphrodite."

"Big word," Gary said. "Mr. Turturici will just love you, dear."

"Asshole," Burr said and flung himself upon Gary. They wrestled around a bit. Jimmy looked at me, and I looked at Jimmy. We were best friends and realized that something else was happening to our lives that summer besides our own boyhood.

"I've got it," I declared.

"Hey, you guys," Jimmy said. He shoved the rolling mass of twelve-year-old flesh. "C'mon, knock it off."

Burr and Gary sat up.

"Listen," I said, "why don't we go over to the drugstore and swipe the new copy of *Playboy?*"

The idea left my friends speechless. We had not had to resort to lifting those glossy gardens of earthly delight. My older brother Frank had come home from the navy, and his subscription had followed. It was true that we could only sneak glances when he was out of the house, but that had seemed enough. The desire to possess such treasure, however, had of late been growing strong within me.

"Yeah," Jimmy laughed.

"We could stash it out in my barn," Burr said. "Oh, mama."

"Old man Hawkins catches us, he'll never let us in the drugstore again," said Gary.

The thought gave us pause. Ernie Smithers had been nabbed last Halloween lifting bags of miniature Hershey bars in Hawkins's drugstore and had not been allowed to return, but Ernie was goofy; he had fallen out of a tree when he was little and had been held back in the third grade.

"Let's do it," Jimmy said. "What the hell."

"What the hell," I agreed.

"We'll need a gimmick," said Jimmy. "The old bastard watches us like a hawk."

"Some reason why we're in there," Burr said, because nobody had any money.

"Hey, maybe your mom will make us malted milk shakes again," Gary suggested. There were stools along the counter in the drugstore, and right across the aisle from the counter was the magazine rack.

We looked at Jimmy. His face was blank, but he was thinking. Six years ago his folks had been separated. Strictly speaking, Jimmy's father just left one night and didn't come back. Jimmy's mother never finished high school, and there isn't much work in town and she wanted to get a divorce, but she went to work for old man Hawkins making sandwiches and milk shakes at the fountain and barely made ends meet.

Sometimes Jimmy's father called. Every time it was Jimmy who talked to him. He didn't want to, but his mother left the room when she knew who it was, and Jimmy listened to his father's raspy voice and didn't say much. He wanted to hang up, but the voice was so clear and loud that it sounded as though his father was calling from the Country Pride down the street. For all he knew his father could be a thousand miles away and probably was, but it made no difference, he was standing in that green booth with the broken light just outside the restaurant, and he always asked the same question. "What's your mother doing now, boy?"

And always Jimmy answered, "Nothing."

"She isn't doing nothing, you say?"

"No, nothing."

"I see," his father said and hung up.

A few days later a ten-dollar bill appeared in a small manila envelope addressed to Jimmy, and Jimmy gave the money to his mother, and every time she set the bill on fire with a wooden kitchen match.

Jimmy's father hadn't called for quite awhile now, and his mother was actually going out with a man who had bought the Jessup place just east of town and who came into the drugstore sometimes for pills. His name was Thompson, and he seemed all right, at least Jimmy's mother thought so, because Jimmy said it was the first time he had heard her laugh since he could remember, and, of course, all that made Jimmy feel even worse. I could see him thinking about it.

"Well?" Burr said.

"I don't know," said Jimmy.

"It wouldn't hurt to ask," Gary said. "Would it?"

Jimmy looked at me. "We'll just wait for my brother's copy," I said. "It's no big deal."

"Maybe she'll offer," Gary said, "if we just go in and sit down."

She had done that once, just after the first time she went out with Mr. Thompson.

Jimmy shrugged his shoulders.

We walked along the road toward town. The other two went ahead, but I held back with Jimmy.

"Just get that out of your head now," I said.

"I can't help it," Jimmy said.

"That's just a bunch of shit and you know it," I said. "Your mother would never be like that. You know that."

"Well, it's true."

"It's shit," I said. "You know it's shit."

"If I weren't there, she could do something."

"I don't want to hear it."

"Well, it's true."

"Shut up, Jimmy."

"She even said so."

He had told me this a dozen times lately, and it scared me every time I heard it. "She was just pissed, that's all. Parents say things when they're pissed. They don't mean it when they say it. So cut it out."

The talk about jumping into Solomon's Pool, it was just hurt talk, the hurt of loneliness and fear all mixed together, the talk of someone whose father had held his fingers against a hot stove when he was three because he had broken a cheap fishing pole and had to learn a lesson, and all the other lessons his father had taught him with a knuckled, hambone fist. I hated Jimmy's father more than I hated my own.

The road went up through pasture land, and there were walnut trees and a house or two. Gary and Burr picked up rocks and threw them at fence posts. After awhile we came to three gnarled oaks, and there was Willie Barlow's old place, sitting back in a bunch of weeds and shrubs. Jimmy stopped.

"What are you doing?" I asked.

"Haven't you wondered?" he said.

We stared. Vines crept against the house, sending fingers here and there to touch the eaves, where the brown paint rolled away in curled, dry flakes. The bricks of the chimney had loosened, and the shingles of the roof were tipped and gray and stringy. Old people in town said that Willie Barlow had been a doctor and saved a lot of lives somewhere but had quit and moved here a long time ago. They said he was crazy, but Mr. Hawkins had started taking medicine out to the place, and he had told Jimmy's mother that old man Barlow was no more crazy that Reverend Chisholm, who was old too and still ran the Methodist church. No one knew why he was here, but if he wanted to keep to himself, he had picked a good place for it. Long before we had grown up enough to creep about the place at night, trying to look through the windows to measure the quality of adventure by the depth of our fear, old man Barlow had become as distant, as alien, and as mysterious to us as the processions that left Martin's Funeral Home on Oak Street and moved slowly through the heart of town to the cemetery at the top of the hill.

Jimmy stepped to the iron gate that closed the road from the house.

"I don't care what he looks like," I said. "Come on. Let's go."

"Not what he looks like," Jimmy said. "He'd look like any other old crud, wouldn't he? But what does he do, that's what I mean. What would someone who lived by himself all that time do?"

"He's too old to do anything."

"Think of it. He doesn't have anybody and nobody has him. He doesn't need friends. I should live here."

"You're nuts."

"Yeah," he said. "Willie Barlow and Jimmy Murphy."

"Hey, for chrissake, what are you doing?"

Jimmy raised the latch of the gate.

"I'm going to go see."

"See what? Jimmy. Jesus. Come back here."

But Jimmy crept forward and disappeared behind the bushes and vines.

By this time Gary and Burr had returned. They stood beside me.

"What are you guys doing?" Burr asked. "Where's Jimmy?"

I pointed.

"Jesus," they said.

We pressed our bodies against the gate and stared at the weathered old house. It was the first time I truly thought that Jimmy might kill himself.

Ten minutes went by, but it was as long as waiting for recess. Then he appeared. He stood just outside the shrubs looking at us. Slowly he walked over. His face was empty. I never saw a face like that. I opened the gate and he came through.

"What happened?" I asked.

Jimmy shook his head.

"Did you see him?" Gary asked. "Did you see old man Barlow?"

He nodded.

"Well, what was he like? What was he doing?" We pressed around, touching his arms and shoulders.

"He wasn't doing anything," Jimmy said. "I peeked in a window, and there was this man who must be a thousand years old. He was just sitting in a chair."

"That's all?" I said. "That's everything."

"There was this picture on a table, and he was crying."

Nobody talked anymore the rest of the way into town. When we got to the drugstore, Jimmy opened the door, and we followed him inside. His mother was behind the counter washing dishes. Mr. Hawkins was nowhere in sight.

Jimmy's mother was better looking than mine and younger too. She had light brown hair that she used to let go, but now she combed it up, and it was shiny and thick and there were curls just above the temples. Everybody felt sorry for her, which only made it tougher on Jimmy, and my father said if things were so bad, why didn't she just move out of town and start somewhere else, which I thought was stupid and mean. She had big eyes, and when she smiled, you couldn't believe that anybody would do to her what Jimmy's father had done.

We went to the counter and sat on the stools. She looked at us and said, "Hello, boys, what have you been up to today?"

"Nothing," Jimmy said.

She nodded and gave him one of those looks.

"It's hot outside," said Gary, who was always thinking.

"Yes, I imagine it is."

"Sure works up a thirst," Gary said.

"Would you boys like something cold to drink?" she asked.

"We sure would, Mrs. Murphy," Burr said.

She fetched four glasses off the rack behind her, dropped in some chipped ice, filled the glasses with water, and set them down before us.

"Excuse me, boys."

She went to the far end of the counter. Mr. Thompson was standing behind the shelves of vitamins. She leaned over and began talking to him.

We drank the water and went outside. I honestly think she would have fixed us the milk shakes finally if we'd asked, particularly since Mr. Thompson had shown up and made her smile. It didn't matter. When we got down the street, Jimmy pulled a copy of the magazine out from under his shirt.

That night I asked my mother if I could sleep over at Jimmy's. It wasn't just that he had our glossy copy of earthly delight hidden under his mattress. I had felt strange and scared all afternoon.

We had pork chops and cheese potatoes for dinner. Jimmy's mother is a good cook. We helped with the dishes, and after awhile Mr. Thompson came over and Jimmy's mother said why didn't we go on up to Jimmy's room, which is just what we wanted anyway, and Mr. Thompson and Jimmy's mother sat in the living room watching television. At ten o'clock we stopped talking dirty, turned off the light, and went to sleep.

It was around twelve that the row started. We were awakened by a yell, and something crashed downstairs. When we got there, Jimmy's mother was on the floor and her mouth was bleeding, and Jimmy's father was standing over her.

She held out her hand. "Get out of here," she said to Jimmy. "Get away from here."

Jimmy ran straight for his father and butted him in the stomach. Jimmy's father was short and squat, and it hardly blew the wind out of him. He was more surprised than anything. Jimmy's mother was surprised, too, and it took her a moment to scream and when she did, Jimmy's father swung at Jimmy with the back of his hand, sending him sprawling across the sofa, and I ran upstairs and called the sheriff.

When I got back downstairs, Jimmy's father was gone and Jimmy's mother was sitting in a chair crying. It seems Jimmy's father had waited outside for Mr. Thompson to leave and then knocked on the door, and Jimmy's mother had opened it, thinking Mr. Thompson had forgotten something. The sheriff caught Jimmy's father ten miles out on the Carson Mine Road, just where it meets the interstate.

In a little while Mr. Thompson came back, and he sat next to Jimmy's mother with his arm around her. All he said was, "I'll never leave you again, Tess, I'll never leave you again."

And Jimmy's mother looked at Jimmy.

Jimmy went upstairs and began getting dressed. It was past one o'clock.

"Hey," I said.

Jimmy didn't say anything, but his face was terrible.

"Come on," I said. "He can't hurt anybody ever again. Let's go to bed now, Jim."

But he laced up his shoes and stood before me. "You can come," he said, "or you can stay here."

"Jim, come on."

He moved to the window.

"All right," I said, "all right. Wait a minute."

I pulled on my clothes, and we climbed out into the elm tree that grew beside the house. When we hit the ground, Jim made off straight-away.

I was scared plenty now and didn't know what to say. He was big-ger and stronger, and I knew I couldn't stop him unless I hit him with something, which I decided I would do if I had to.

Everything in town was dark, and we walked right out and headed for the road we had taken that morning. Then we picked up the Southern Pacific Railroad tracks.

"Let's just talk awhile," I said. "Jim, all right? Mr. Thompson's a nice guy. He likes you. He likes you more than you think, I'll bet. Hell, he likes the whole gang, really. I wish he were my father."

"I've got it figured out now," he said. "I know just how to do it."

"Hey, come on, Jim."

"You saw her face."

"That doesn't mean anything. She was just scared. You can't blame her for being scared, can you?"

"What difference does it make? I'm in the way, that's all. I'm al-ways in the way."

He walked on ahead, and I began looking around for something to pick up.

When we got to the bridge, the moon was above the hills. Every-thing was shadow, covered by a pale glaze of light. The river below looked much deeper, and the riffles beyond churned the darkness into a gray froth before working down into the black trees beyond.

"Rocks," Jimmy said.

He stood pointing. The sound of the river met his outstretched hand.

Jimmy stepped along the trestle to the embankment and scrambled over. I followed, my hands fumbling in the brush. When we got to the water's edge, he began filling his pockets.

"I'll stuff them into my shirt too," he said. "Then I'll climb back up." He turned to me. "Maybe you should go."

All I could say was his name.

"I'm not scared," he said. "I'm going to do it."

He turned his back and I found a good-sized rock and got behind him. I lifted it with both hands, but as I brought it down, he moved and the thing glanced off the side of his head and caught him on the shoulder. I heard something crack, and he screamed in pain.

"You sonofabitch!" he yelled.

"You can't kill yourself!" I yelled back. "You're my best friend, and I won't let you kill yourself!"

He was on his feet and staggering toward me. I retreated downstream. "It's my life, goddamnit, and I'll kill myself if I want to! It's my life, you sonofabitch!"

I stumbled a few yards further and stopped. In a small back eddy of the river something was sticking out of the water. Jimmy came up beside me. We stared. It was a head. We watched it turn this way and that.

We pulled the body out onto the bank as far as we could. Little currents came from it. Neither of us had ever seen anyone dead before.

"Jesus," Jimmy said. "It's Willie Barlow."

He was old, all right. In the pale darkness he was much older than I had imagined, and with his silent blue face, stringy white hair, and his legs still in the water, he was more mysterious, distant, and alien than ever before.

"Jim," I said, "I didn't want to hit you with that rock."

He came over to stand very close to me. He looked at the railroad bridge silhouetted against the night sky.

"I'll never kill myself again," he said.

He held his arm and began to cry. We stood in the moonlight looking at the dead man.

The Shopper

When his wife died, John Tilden sold the house and moved into an apartment across town. It was a nice apartment near a neighborhood park like those one finds scattered through every city. A bus stopped at the corner.

A market was down the street, and he went there for the packaged meats and frozen vegetables. He always walked because he had never had to shop for himself, and walking the two blocks made his entry into the market a little more natural.

He pushed a cart down the aisles and stared at the shelves of useless things he did not know and would never use. He looked at everything, amazed and frightened by all the names, all the cartons and bottles and cans with ingredients written in a language he could not understand. Was this what his dead wife, Elaine, had mastered, while he spent those years making files at the office? He found a new appreciation for her in the market, lost in a jungle of liquid and flour, like an explorer without a guide. There was something forbidden about it.

He learned right away to spot those who, like himself, lived alone. They took a stick of butter from a package. They bought a quart of milk. There was a bar or two of soap and a single loaf of bread. They broke bananas into groups of three and slipped one bunch of radishes into a plastic bag, even when they were four for a dollar. One filet, and toilet tissue by the roll. They pushed their carts quickly down the aisles, and the things bumped across the steel mesh. They knew just what they wanted.

After a few weeks he came to recognize some of the shoppers, and the checkout girl named Susan smiled and said hello. The market became less intimidating when he realized they always put everything in the same place.

He was amazed by the young mothers, shopping in pairs and pulling a child or two. Their baskets would burst to overflowing, and they bought more of everything and always in the large sizes. When they stood in front of him at the register, they unfolded coupons like bank tellers and wrote checks for two hundred dollars. Then twelve days later, there they'd be again, pushing another mountain of food.

There were husbands who handled baskets for their wives, trailing behind them, blank-faced and sullen, as the women searched along the shelves and said just how many of this or that to pull down. There were men with long lists, leaving carts in the middle of the aisles, cursing among the cans and boxes because their wives were working too, and someone would pretend to be an automobile horn and say, "You're blocking traffic."

And he carried his bag of groceries home.

It was difficult learning to live alone, and for a time he did not sleep well. He had not realized it, but, lying next to Elaine, he had grown accustomed to a certain kind of darkness. At their house the bedroom was located at the rear, and there were no outside lights, and when he crawled into bed, a blackness came upon the room that was so final it seemed there could be nothing but sleep.

Here the bedroom was located at the front, and the amber glow of the streetlamp lay like oil on the ceiling and floor. When a car went by, a light appeared against the near wall, crept slowly away and then, narrowing, disappeared in a streak through the far corner of the room.

He lost friends, of course, though they invited him for a time. He sat on the print sofas, sipping dry martinis and trying to smile. The conversation was abstract: aid to the Contras, the bombing of abortion clinics. They couldn't hold it for long, though. Life pulled them back. Where were Ted and Ellen going next weekend? Had the decorator finished the design for the new kitchen? What were they all doing for the holiday?

Then they noticed him, perched alone, with an empty glass in his hand, and grew embarrassed. He had never realized before how important it was to be someone's husband. The same thing happened when you were divorced. It had happened to Ed and Lorraine Shelby last year and Randy and Helene Goodman the year before. They just dropped out of life, and you met them sometimes for lunch downtown, but they never came to dinner and they never went with you to the lake.

Only it was worse when your wife died. That made them downright uncomfortable. They kept you around for a time because they felt sorry, but there was something terrible and strange about you now, as though you had contracted a disease. Divorce brought no finality, even if it was your fault. But with death someone was taken out of the world, and there would always be an empty plate.

He was lonely. There was no question about that. A house full of undusted furniture. The echo of footsteps in a room when the television is off. The light at evening that clings to the saucer and cup. These things cast him down. But he wondered, was it a condition caused by a missing wife, or had he, all those years, lived under a disguise?

A few friends, motivated, he imagined, by real affection, but more probably by a need to reaffirm balance, tried to get women for him. He found himself passing pepper steak or spinach soufflé to ebullient females who had spent the afternoon at the hairdresser's and smelled suspiciously like the perfume counter at Macy's.

He went out with some of the women, who were divorced or widowed. They sat in the restaurants and talked of their children. He tried to smile and seem curious, but after a time the conversations ran together, and he was afraid to ask questions for fear of making a mistake.

Elaine and he had not gone out much after the first years, and he realized, as the dinners went by, that he had lived a conventional life. Was it wrong to enjoy staying home to a meal that you could eat with your slippers on? And if the world passed you by, of what importance was that? He got enough of it on the evening news. In the end the world didn't matter anyway. Nothing mattered but the echo inside your own brain. And so he picked one of the women, the nicest one, to his thinking, and he went to her place or she came to his, and there began to appear on the dinner table again all those things he had missed for a time. Life settled back around him.

He had shopped in the store a month before he noticed the woman with the black hair. He did not understand at first. He guessed she was a regular from the way the clerks spoke to her at the checkout counter. Then he realized that he never saw her in the aisles of dry cereal and canned vegetables. It was only when Eleanor began asking him to pick up cocoa beans or cinnamon sticks that he found her, alone at the rear of the store, turning over strange, pastel cartons that were printed in foreign tongues.

She was quite attractive, not young by any means, but certainly not so old as he. She was someplace in between, where all dark women linger for a time. She was beautiful. He could say that, glimpsing her out of the corner of his eye as he fumbled among the odd-shaped bottles with the strange aromas. But he had known beautiful women, truly beautiful, so that you thought their pictures might have appeared in magazines, or you might have known them in school. She was beautiful, but not spontaneously so, until that first time—it was not the first day he saw her—when she looked into his eyes, and then he thought she was perhaps the most beautiful woman he had ever seen.

There was a manner about her, unhurried but deliberate, as though she were choosing only those things needed for a journey. She was always neatly dressed, darkly, conservatively, but with some color about the throat, a scarf or handkerchief or something pinned above the breast, and when she walked, she placed one foot directly before the other, as though moving along a precipice. This action made her hips turn in a particular way, which contrasted with her aloof self-assurance, and he thought she must certainly be Eastern, Turkish or Lebanese, perhaps. He had seen that movement before on a television program filmed in a bazaar in Damascus.

But what surprised him more than anything was that she walked to the market as well. He turned one day to see her across the street, looking straight ahead, a tiny black purse clutched in her hand. He was able to get in the checkout line behind her and hurried after her when he was done. She was already down the street on the opposite side, a brown paper bag in her arms. She turned off at the first intersection and went away from him. He paused a moment, pretending to shift his bag of groceries, and watched that steady, careful step move along the edge of the world.

His life became more comfortable with the passing days. He had never realized the importance of continuity before, but seeing Eleanor there, bent over the kitchen counter, arranging ingredients into a special order which inevitably produced a flavorful, hearty meal, was like finding all his shirts clean and pressed and buttoned at the collar. He enjoyed clearing the table for her and standing at the sink while she washed and he dried, or just sitting in the living room, the sound of the stereo coming quietly from the wall, while she sewed or turned the pages of a magazine and he read the evening paper. Gradually his shoulders dropped a bit and the stiffness in his neck lessened. Several times, after a heavy dinner, he found her shaking him gently when the eight o'clock movie was done. He had fallen asleep with the paper across his chest.

She was a fine woman, gentler than Elaine had been and with much more patience. He did not know if he should attribute this to maturity—he had married Elaine when he was twenty-one—nevertheless, he was gratified that certain things no longer needed to be worked out, that she was content to be who she was and allow him the same privilege.

"Do you think it means we're over the hill?" he had joked one night at the table.

"What do you mean?" she had laughed in return.

"You know, so busy going down the other side that it's all we can do to hold on."

"Why, John, what a strange thought. You're still a young man."

He smiled and felt vaguely proud. "We do enjoy being together, don't we?" he said, refilling her wine glass.

"I enjoy these moments more than you can know," she replied.

"Yes," he said.

"Our quiet evenings together."

He lifted his glass and set it down.

"Are you happy?" he asked.

She looked at him. "Yes," she said, "I am."

"It really isn't a mysterious or complicated thing, is it?"

"No," she said.

"It's really quite simple."

"Would you like another roll?" she asked.

He took the rolls, touching her fingers beneath the basket.

"I thought when my wife died that I had lost something forever."

"Yes," she said. "Pain can be confusing."

He did not say anything, and the music floated in from the living room.

But he remembered what his mother had said—she had turned her sunken face toward him on the gray pillow, but her eyes had been closed—just before her death: "Only the old can truly leave life alone." And he was confused.

Was it love? he wondered. In age did love come to you out of loneliness and not passion, as it did in youth? Was it love he was beginning to feel for Eleanor Madden?

And then one evening they were invited to dinner at the Pattersons', where they had met, and there, leaning upon the white tablecloth as the veal and rice moved by him in the china bowls Helen Patterson had used for years and the antique clock in the hall chimed in that odd, porcelain way, he felt such a strange apprehension that he excused himself and went to the upstairs bathroom. He was there for ten minutes, splashing his cheeks and looking at himself in the egg-shaped mirror. He looked at the bayberry candle Helen always burned in a tray on the toilet cover. He looked at the little blue soaps and the blue hand towels. He could not tell if the eyes in the mirror looked too, for when he turned back, they were staring at him.

He flushed the toilet and went back to the table. They were talking about trips, and as he sat down, Eleanor said that she was leaving the following Sunday to visit her sister upstate for a week.

He drove her to the airport and stood in the waiting area until it was time for her to board. She kissed him and said, "Goodbye, darling. I'll see you next Sunday."

"I'll be here," he said, patting her shoulder.

"I left a surprise for you in the refrigerator," she said. "I hope you like it."

He smiled and said, "Thank you."

She walked down the boarding platform, and he went to the window. He watched the plane move off and then taxi to the runway. He watched it come down the runway in a long, metal line and then lift into the air. The plane went up and turned away. He watched it become only a dark point in the blue, northern sky. Then it disappeared. He felt relieved.

The following day he did not go to work. Instead he stayed in the apartment puttering about until eleven, when he went over to Eleanor's to check the mail, take in the paper, and feed the cat. He did these things because he had said he would. It was true that he did not mind doing them. Yet, to find Samantha, the black-eared Siamese, come toward to him in recognition, made him uneasy. Were they already so familiar that she trusted him with a key and the free run of all her earthly possessions?

He stood in the kitchen listening to the cat purr over its tuna bits. The day was overcast—there was rain predicted for the end of the week—and a wan light fell along the formica counter. The house had never been so quiet. He opened the refrigerator. On the top shelf was a casserole dish with a note taped to the lid. The note said, "Enjoy."

He closed the refrigerator door. His heart was pounding. He went into the dining room and opened the buffet drawers. Then he went into the hall and opened the cupboards.

He walked into the bathroom and pulled the drawers and then

stepped into the bedroom. There was a pleasant scent and the light was faint because the curtains were drawn. He opened all the chests and looked at the contents. He went into the closet and looked at that. Then he went to the bed and sat down.

In a moment the cat came in and jumped up beside him. He did not touch it but it purred anyway. He sat on the bed with the cat and could not understand what he had done and why he was afraid. Then the cat stopped purring and curled up to sleep. He stayed there a long time watching the cat sleeping.

The following evening he went out to dinner. There was a new place in town, The Café Armand, and he didn't particularly like going to restaurants alone but he went anyway. They put him next to a potted palm and a fountain that poured water over white marble. A waiter in a black waistcoat handed him a menu, and he ordered something called *Caneton à l'Orange Armand.* The wine steward suggested a chilled white Burgundy.

It was a very pleasant place, with plants hanging about and very soft light that dripped mysteriously from the ceiling. There were tiny lamps with green shades on every table. The steward returned with the wine and was very meticulous with the cork. He sipped the wine and liked it and the steward smiled and left, and then he sat alone drinking.

There was music in the room. It seemed to come up through the floor, muted by the lush carpet, and swirl about his legs. Above his head was the tinkle of conversation and silverware. The air seemed clearly divided into light, voices, and music. He smiled and looked at the people.

There were earnest, young couples who sat in pairs, and the men, suit coats off, still talked of business, while the wives, who had had time to get ready, leaned over the table and touched each other as they spoke. There were women together and men and several white-haired couples, who must have tried all the good places in town and were now trying this one. There were no children.

He felt strange, like a crow in a brood of starlings, and he was thankful for the food when it arrived.

He had begun the entrée when he looked up to see the maitre d' escorting the dark-haired woman from the market to a small table against the far wall.

She wore a black dress and a white scarf. Her hair was pulled straight back, which made the angles of her face appear sharper and more brilliant. In all his life he had never seen a more beautiful woman.

She sat down facing away from him but so that he could see the line of her jaw and the curve of her mouth. Not once did she look about the room. Even after the waiter took her order, she remained within herself, as though seated at the theater. She placed her hands upon the table cloth, and when the steward brought a glass of wine, she took a sip and allowed the fingers of one hand to embrace the stem.

He experienced now a sensation so strange and compelling that it frightened him with its intensity. He had to resist standing up. He wanted to go over to the table and sit down opposite her. He wanted to ask her name, ask anything he might think of. He could not take his eyes away.

"Is something wrong, Sir?" he heard a voice say at his elbow.

"Wrong?" he said, looking up.

"Your dinner, Sir," the waiter said. "Is it not satisfactory?"

He glanced at his plate, where the brown sauce had taken on a kind of glazed, dull sheen. "Oh, no," he said. "It's fine." He had hardly touched it. "Really, it's quite good."

The waiter backed away, trying to smile, and when he was gone, John Tilden threw some bills onto the tablecloth and, keeping his eyes straight ahead and with more embarrassment than he wanted to admit, left The Café Armand.

He went back to his apartment, got dressed for bed, and turned off the lamp. Immediately the room was filled with an amber glow. He lay staring at the ceiling. A car came up the street, and a pale white light appeared against the wall. He watched it move away and then vanish into the corner. He got up, put on his clothes and went over to Eleanor's to sleep with the cat.

The following day he walked to the market and she was there. He was amazed to think that a place like this could contain such a woman and the ingredients for banana nut bread.

He stood apart from her, pretending to look through the bottles of colored spice. She was turning over the pastel cartons. He could just smell her perfume.

As he watched her out of the corner of his eye, a giddiness filled him. The sound of piano and violins that came always from the walls of the market and to which he had grown completely immune now took on an odd poignancy, like the music in an old film.

In his mind she belonged to no one, a single person who, from birth, had been cast out upon the vagaries of life. Bitter at first, wretched and without hope, she had lived in one place after another, a child-hood lost among cousins and aunts. In the most abject loneliness, her beauty had emerged, like a rose among the weeds, and jealousy had come to the families. She had been sent away to school.

In school she had found books and the glory of imagination. Later when she was older and there were boys, they always rode behind the fair men who galloped across the pages that she read. And even passion, when it arrived and departed and then arrived and departed again, left her truly as it had found her, prepared to move on.

Then the war came, filling the world with such pain that only the bravest or most foolhardy might survive. Violence and death lay on every side. The families were rent asunder, and when she went to them, they drew comfort from her courage, her insurmountable strength, and, in her silent heart, she was grateful to them for not having loved her, so that she might endure all this lovelessness.

And then, as she wandered among the victims and the disconsolate, she found the young man. Such sweetness they snatched from the cannon's mouth! Such joy they plucked from the machine gun's rattle! In the midst of nothing they had themselves, and even when he was lost forever on some killing field, she was thankful that, at the end of everything, standing alone on the tarmac waiting for the plane to America, there had been love.

Transfixed, he looked at her. The music faded into the walls. Like survivors, they stood queued up for passage to another shore. When she glanced at him, he turned his face away in shame and desire.

She moved toward the checkout counter, and he followed, pulling things here and there from the shelves and dropping them into his basket. He trailed behind, allowing a shopper to step between them, and when he finally got out the door, she was already a quarter of a block down the street on the other side. He hurried, waiting until she turned at the intersection before he crossed against the red light.

He stayed fifty paces behind her, stepping on the balls of his feet. Staring at her measured tread, he felt as though he too were balancing on the edge of the world.

Halfway down the block, she turned into a path that led to a rather plain house, with xylosma and hawthorn planted about the foundation. There was a single willow tree growing in front. He passed by hurriedly, lifting the bag of groceries to his chin, and was startled to find a *For Sale* sign stuck into the lawn.

Flushed and confused, he walked home, put the things away and went over to Eleanor's. He took the casserole from the refrigerator and spooned half of it down the disposal.

At the end of the week she returned from her sister's. He went to the airport to meet her. The first thing she wanted to know after he had embraced her and taken her bag was, had he fed the cat?

In the car she said, "I told my sister about us. She's thrilled and delighted."

That evening, over a meal of roast pork, spinach, and hot bread, they talked about being married.

Really, this place was big enough, she suggested. He could leave his tiny apartment and come over here. They would buy new bedroom furniture. They would put up new wallpaper. He listened and agreed to everything.

That night he awoke from a troubled sleep to find two yellow eyes peering at him in the darkened room. He sat up, terrified, and slid his feet off the bed. The eyes did not move. He stood, trembling, and there was a little muffled sound and something landed on the carpet. It was the cat. It had been sitting on the dresser next to the door.

He stood for a time next to Eleanor's bed and listened to her breathing. Gradually his heart slowed, but a dull weight was pressed upon his chest. He tiptoed to the chair, picked up his clothes, and went into the kitchen.

The cat was lapping at its milk. He tried to be amused at how it had frightened him. Yet, when it lifted its head and stared at him, the fear returned. Something in its eyes seemed sent from the underworld to befuddle him. Slowly he dressed and tried not to think of his life, not to think of it all at one time, as he had done in those black hours after Elaine's death. It was not good to think of life as a complete thing. It was better to live it in fragments, one piece at a time.

He left quietly, got into his car, and drove to the apartment. Then he walked up the street to the intersection. It was cold and damp, and the weatherman was right because he could see no stars. There would be rain generally everywhere.

He stood on the sidewalk before the woman's house. A light was on behind a drawn shade. Perhaps, even now, she was packing.

Hadn't something been promised him long ago, in childhood, when there seemed a kind of limitlessness to life? Wasn't there some freedom greater than the decision about what to have for dinner or where to go for the summer holiday?

He stood shivering in the night air, trying to make up his mind. He wanted to go up to her door. He wanted to ask her to please take him with her. Wherever she was going, he wanted to go too. And it didn't matter if he ever came back again.

Pale Morning Dun

That evening we crawled under the fence and looked at the house where old man Fario had died. Wooden slats were nailed over the windows and the front door was padlocked. The grass was brown like the weeds along the road. Some of the branches were dead on the willow tree.

"What do you think?" I asked.

Jerry looked at me and smiled. "No problem." He found a stick, broke it in half, put one piece between his teeth and handed me the other. We slithered forward on our bellies like Chuck Norris in the movie playing at the Bijou in Livingston.

We got across the dead grass, past the willow tree and Jerry held up a hand. I stopped, bit down on the combat knife, my ear cocked against the sounds of the jungle.

"What is it?" I said.

"I heard something."

The wind came up from the meadow where the stream ran. It lifted the American flag old man Fario always kept poking from the house. The stripes rolled, turned over, and fell limp, like a wide red-and-white fly line. Something in the roof creaked.

The house had stood out here for as long as anyone could remember. The somber gray, which you see painted on a lot of the old places, was gone, the wood, slivered and bleached. Two pillars held up an arch over the front steps. In the late afternoon, with the sun behind the cottonwood trees, it looked like the entrance to a cave or the deep, dark water beneath an undercut bank. Over the years, coming up from the stream along the dirt road toward home, we had seen a figure, wavering there in the gloom.

We were curious about him. Because he never went to town, never, as far as anyone knew, even left the house—food, medicine, and an occasional shirt or pair of boots drifting in to him from the stores along Front Street—he was mysterious and untouchable.

Now he was gone, disappeared to that deeper mystery, about which few ever spoke, even on Sunday, to which our own Grandpa Alan had gone one evening last year while Jerry and I were knee-deep in Horseman's Run. Gramp loved to fly-fish, even when his eyes got so bad he couldn't see the tiny imitation riding the crest of Horseman's Run, and Gram had to stand just out of his casting arc to tell him when to strike. He taught Jerry and me all we knew about trout, the patient, gentle rhythm of fly casting and the faithfulness of releasing everything we caught. The evening after Gramp disappeared I fully expected he would come in from the hill where he always went to watch the sunset and take his place next to my mother.

We studied the house, hunkered down in the dry grass and weeds. We had no idea why anyone would board up the windows and fasten a lock to the front door of such a lonely place, unless it was to keep us out. This was, of course, the thinking of boys, who believe that life coincides with their passage upon the current of time, for hadn't we often hidden our rods and crept about the perimeter of the house, hatching a plan of attack, but prepared always for flight?

"I don't hear anything," I said.

There were underground storage rooms. We had observed the old man remove the chain, throw open the heavy wooden door, descend invisible steps, and vanish beneath the house. It was then that we were at our boldest, crawling up to peer over into the emptiness and gloom. We never saw him. But we heard him—scrapings and grind-ings and the thick sound of things being moved, and his voice, low and muttering. We were amused that, deep down in the dark, the old man talked to himself.

We made our way round to the side, the odd calls from the jungle, the grotesque shapes of dying trees, the ashen fortress itself rising above us more dangerous than anything Chuck Norris faced, far back in enemy territory.

The cellar door was locked. Jerry grabbed the rusted chain and shook it. From the hollow below a sound returned, met itself, fell back, returned again. Jerry struck the door. The sound came with a growl, collapsed, mounted the stairs, moaned against the heavy wood, disappeared.

"There's no way in," I said. "Come on."

"Maybe we could climb up," Jerry said, pointing to the second story. "Maybe there's a window or something."

"And maybe this isn't such a good idea after all. They don't want anybody around here, Jer."

"Who doesn't? Mom says there aren't any relatives. They can't find anybody to do the funeral."

"Well, somebody put up the boards and those locks."

"The sheriff, probably."

An older brother is an ambiguous thing. He goes first and shows the way, but he also charts paths into trouble.

"I don't know," I said.

"Well, what would Chuck do?"

I grinned. "Fall back and reconnoiter?"

He punched my arm and stood up. "We've been doing that for years. Come on."

We had never seen the back of the house. It was concealed from the road, which dropped off sharply to the stream, and by the time we got up and by, a stand of cottonwoods blocked the view.

The decay was worse. Spring rains always revived the front yard with wildflowers and sent out occasional willow shoots below the branches which had died the summer before, so that coming along the road, we found even the dark place beneath the portico less forbidding. But here the ground had been scraped so that not a blade of grass grew. Broken pieces of machinery were strewn about, rusted into the earth like iron bones. Beneath the rear windows were stacks of packing crates, their ends split open, boxes of electric motors, broken appliances, and power tools: he had earned money by fixing things. There was only one door, and it too was locked.

"Goddamnit," Jerry said.

A few paces from the back door was a fire pit. I went over to have a look while Jerry studied the house for a way in. Around the pit were a few charred embers, bits of blackened metal and glass. A rusty gas can sat next to the pit on a block of wood. I kicked at the ashes. Something turned over and caught my eye. I picked it up. It was a perfectly white shirt button of a kind I'd seen all my life. The center holes where the thread goes were broken.

"Hey, Tom," Jerry called.

He was stacking some of the smaller boxes on top of one of the crates.

"That screen up there," he said, "I don't think it's fastened. Come on."

The light had begun to fade. The air was getting damp. The dust we had kicked up hovered above the ground. Beyond, in the trees that obscured the house from the road, shadows pressed together. The edge of things was gone. It was the time when sound does not rise but spreads, like voices across a stream, yet there was no sound, not the slightest murmur, even from far away. I looked at Jerry. He floated upon the dust, hands on hips, watching me. I looked back into the trees. A bell had come down over us.

"Mom will be fixing dinner," I said. "We'd better get in."

"We'll tell her the afternoon hatch was late and they were rising like crazy. She won't care. Help me here."

We made a pile of rubbish on the crate, and Jerry kneed his way to the top. He squatted a moment, then stood slowly erect. "There's a piece of rope in that box by the door," he said. "Grab it."

When I returned, he had already lifted the screen and was raising the window.

"Wait a second," I said, "Jerry," but his legs vanished over the sill. It was a full five minutes before I saw him again. I knew what he was doing. Sometimes on the stream I'd look back and he'd be around a bend fishing on his own. He didn't care anything about how I felt when I expected to find him and he wasn't there.

Then his head came out. "Wait'll you see this," he said. "Throw me the rope. I'll help you."

I shinnied up the house and dropped inside. It was a small, square room like a bedroom, but it was bare, not a stick of furniture, not even a rug. A door led into a hallway. Jerry went through and I followed.

The other rooms upstairs were empty too. The bathrooms had no towels or soap or anything to make you think they were used.

"What'd I tell you," Jerry said.

We crept down the stairs. There was a large, open space that looked right at the front door. Through the dirty windows on either side I could just see the fence where the road was.

"It's filthy in here," I said.

Dust was on the tables and chairs, the curtains and lamps. When you took a step, a pillow of gray rose from the floor. There were no pictures on the walls, no photographs on the counters, none of that stuff people have strewn around. We went through all the rooms, and all the rooms were the same. It was as though someone had not lived there but only floated about.

"Let's go," I said. "This is creepy."

"But where'd he sleep?" Jerry asked.

In the kitchen the sink was bare, not a glass or a cup. A door was at the far end. Jerry went over and opened it.

It was a small room, like a porch. Inside was a stool and a cushion in which there was a deep impression. Before the stool was a brass telescope, shining softly in the fading light. Certainly the old man had some consolation, then, for the house stood above the most beautiful place in the world. Another door was off to one side, and Jerry tried the knob.

"Locked," he said. "Must be the cellar. I'd sure like to get down there. I wonder if it's the same. He was always shoving stuff around."

I was looking through the telescope. Beyond the cottonwood trees lay the valley of my boyhood. In broad, green swells it rose toward the arrowhead peaks of the mountains. I felt a softness for the old man. A heart that regarded such things could not be dark. I lowered the telescope. A narrow passage had been cut below through the shrubs and limbs. I could see right down to the slick patch of gray and the black arms of the big oak that hung above the water. I stepped back and the stool went to the floor. I pointed. Jerry hurried over and squinted through the lens.

"Jesus," he said. "Horseman's Run."

It seemed that everyone turned out to bury him, as many as turned out for my grandfather's funeral. Mom was forgiving, so Jerry and I went to the stream.

We like to get there before the sun touches the water. Everything is clean and new and fresh, the stones are damp, the air is crisp and clear, the cottonwoods stand green against the sky, the river comes down like blue steel, thudding against the rocks, breaking white over the marbled bottom.

I know now what fly-fishing means, but even then Gramp had taught us to observe. "Don't jump into the water right away, boys," he would say. "Look first, and look right in front of you, against the bank. That's where the big ones lie."

We crept forward, half bent over, our rods behind us. We knew the river as well as we knew our own bedroom. Just here the stream swept round a curve, dropped through a riffle, then opened into a still, dark pool. Below that was Horseman's Run.

"Trout feed ninety percent of the time beneath the surface, boys," Gramp had said. "If you want to catch a lot of fish and big ones, weight your nymphs and bounce them right along the bottom."

He had taught us how to rig up, how to cast, lift the rod, and concentrate on the leader for the slightest hesitation. We had watched him create the dark-bodied bugs that were so effective, for Gramp had studied the river for years. He even taught us how to tie the killer nymphs ourselves, but it was the duns that fascinated us.

"Those nymphs crawl around down there a whole year," he had

said, "before they swim to the surface, break out of their skins, and float along drying their wings. They live only a day more, and that's not long, is it, boys, to be so beautiful."

When Gramp tied those thin-bodied *ephemerella*, as he called them, on size-eighteen hooks, their pale green bodies and diaphanous gray wings reminded us of tiny, unmoored sailboats, and when the duns themselves were adrift upon the surface of the pool, we watched as an entire armada of delicate, translucent ships spun and took flight.

That's when the trout came up, finning easily in the slack currents, their snouts tap-tapping the surface as they took the duns one by one. It was the best time to fly-fish. Everything was there. It was what Jerry and I loved. It was what Gramp, in the end, could no longer see.

"It's still a bit early for the hatch," Jerry said, kneeling in the wet grass above the stream. "Let's put on some nymphs and go down after them."

We rigged up and spread out. I made a couple of false casts and dropped my brown nymph just above the shoulder of a big rock. When the leader skipped sideways, I lifted the rod.

My arm came alive, the weight of the fish throbbed in my hand, the line ran past me and a seventeen-inch rainbow shot out of the water, curving and uncurving, wet silver and pink. "Fish on!" I yelled, the rainbow coming down, shaking its head, the leader popping like thread, everything going slack and no weight. "Lost him," I called, but Jerry was stumbling along the bank, his rod arched dangerously, the line cutting a scratch across the steel blue water. The fish jumped twice. I watched as Jerry did all the things Gramp had shown us. Finally he removed the barbless hook, looked at me, and smiled. I raised my fist. It beat anything Chuck Norris could do.

We fished like that for an hour or so. The sun went to the tops of the trees. The shadows flattened over the river. The air grew warmer, and the dampness left.

"Look!" Jerry shouted.

Sure enough, in the heavy water above were tiny gray sails sculling down to the pool below. I couldn't fish right away. I never can when the duns first come up. I have to watch them, suddenly upon the surface, their wings drying for that one day of life above the stream.

"It's impossible to imitate them truly," Gramp would say, holding one up so that the light shone around the veins in the wings and filled the pale olive body. "Thank God we don't have to, or else we would be obliged to find some way to use them to catch fish, and I don't think we could do that, do you, boys?"

I did not understand then what he meant, but I knew he liked to watch the sails too, and I would find him sometimes, standing alone, smoking his pipe, and staring out over the water. He was the smartest man I ever knew, and it was right to fool trout with delicate imitations. What a surprise it must be to lift up for something so easy to have, only to find the sting in your own mouth. It was good then to remove the hook, hold the fish in the current until it recovered, and let it go, so that it sank down in a remorse that spared a few duns overhead.

I looked over at Jerry, who was busy snipping away the nymph and knotting on a dry fly. Circles had begun to form beneath some of the sails, and the sails disappeared.

The swish-swish of Jerry's line went out over the water and the size-eighteen dun imitation fluttered to the surface directly above a widening ring. The fly drifted, Jerry mended the line, a dark snout showed, the fly vanished, Jerry lifted the rod, and a trout the size of my arm came out of the water and raced downstream. Jerry stumbled and laughed, trying to keep up. A thrill went through me. The duns don't understand or the trout. But everything is caught. Everything is let go. Everything is perfect. Nothing in the whole world is so grand as fly-fishing.

I tied on my imitation, and for two hours Jerry and I worked the long pool and the riffle that dropped toward Horseman's Run. Then we sat on the bank, our feet in the water, and looked up at the sky.

"Chuck doesn't have this," he said.

"No way," I agreed. "There aren't any trout streams in jungles."

He looked downstream to where the big oak hung over the current. "Let's do the Run. It's still good. There will be a few duns. We can find a rise or two."

I looked at the deep, curling water. It was water hard to wade, unbroken at the surface, but heavy and swift. Lunkers held at the

bottom and rose to the duns in the eddies and slicks. The biggest
trout were in Horseman's Run.

"You think we should?" I asked.

"Sure, why not?"

I shrugged, looking up past the oak to the tangle of brush and
limbs.

We stepped down, hunched over into our stalk. A circle formed
near the bank just below the point where shadow met light. Jerry
went to his knees, inched forward, his rod bowed back and forth, the
line whispered above my head, the fly settled to the water, spun a little, caught a seam, then disappeared. In a couple of minutes he had
landed and released a nice rainbow, scanned the water, and then
crawled down to another rise.

I watched, creeping along behind. We came under the black oak.
The few duns that drifted on the Run seemed abandoned and lost.
The fishing was tougher and that was all right, that's how we liked it.
I kept looking up through the branches and brush. There was noth-
ing, but I couldn't fish. I just stared up through the jungle of limbs. I
knew we were there, floating in the center of the lens.

All through high school and into college, when Jerry and I went
away, the old house remained boarded up. We never tried to get inside again, but I was surprised when my brother lost interest in our
most dangerous scheme, to sneak down into old man Fario's cellar.
There were two reasons. Chuck Norris left the Bijou in Livingston,
and Jerry discovered that Judy Sharp, who lived two houses up the
road, was actually a girl. However, as the days passed, I still could not
help stopping a moment each time we walked by, and after awhile,
Jerry, ever more impatient, went along, leaving me to stand alone before that monument to age and decay.

It seemed finally to have stopped changing and to have taken on
the feel of a timeless ruin. The walls, beams, and columns were at last
uniform with whatever weather might do. The roof stopped curling.
The space beneath the portico grew permanently dim. Even the willow trees found neutrality between leaving and staying, the dead

branches as appropriate as those which had managed to live. The house came to inhabit space, much like a large stone or the dark oak above Horseman's Run. After awhile it was just there.

But something did change. Though he went first, my brother and I had always been two faces of one thing. We did everything together, our dreams and hopes, our failures and accomplishments occurring with remarkable consistency. But with Judy Sharp along, Jerry seemed to lose interest in fly-fishing, about which, Gramp had said, there was always more to learn. I found it hard to believe he could drift away like that, but, more often than not, I went to the stream to stalk trout alone.

At first this was intimidating. Jerry and I had a system. When the fishing got tough, we tried different imitations and methods until one of us found something that worked. Now I was left to figure out everything myself, and sometimes, when I cast for hours over water that contained fish, I felt confused and betrayed. Later, when I walked up the road past the old house, I could not stop. I could not even look. Something was there, wavering in the gloom beneath the portico.

But the most remarkable thing happened. I asked Jerry to go fishing with me one morning, which was the only time I had a chance at him because Judy was a late sleeper. He said, sure, we got everything together, even talked strategy, but she called and said she was going shopping with her parents in Livingston, wouldn't he like to come too. And he said, yes, can you believe it, so the next morning I got up before everyone, fixed myself a sandwich and went down to the stream while it was still dark. I was mad, madder than I'd ever been, and I sat on a rock to wait because it was so early I couldn't see the water.

I calmed down after awhile, ate my sandwich; the sky got a little white above the far hills, and that's when it happened. A shiver ran up my back. I felt him standing behind me, there in the trees, smoking his pipe, his fly rod leaning against a stump. He was waiting too for the sun to come over the steel blue water. And his voice said, "Be patient. Sit and watch. Don't always be in a hurry."

The sky grew lighter. The surface of the stream appeared beneath a soft glow. I heard a splash, then another. Trout were rising, but I couldn't see them. Then the color of the current separated from the dark, far bank. More splashes, but now I could see, and there was nothing, no duns, nothing, but the splashes were everywhere, the trout were feeding, but on something I couldn't see. I bent over, put my face right on the surface, the splashes went on, the trout were eating something that wasn't there. I took off my hat and held it in the current. Against the band appeared tiny gray worms with the stubs of half-formed wings. Nothing that Gramp had tied was anything like them.

I looked back at the trees. Had he truly been there, I wouldn't have been surprised, for I felt closer to him at that moment than ever I had before. There was a dimension to fly-fishing I had never imagined. That morning, as long as they allowed, I sat watching trout feed on invisible bugs.

The next day I went with my mother on her weekly trip into town to buy groceries and asked her to drop me at the library. She couldn't have been happier, of course, thinking that I had finally gotten serious about school, but the books I was looking for were books about fly-fishing and fly tying, and I found one about entomology and put it conspicuously atop the stack I checked out. Mom pronounced the word silently in the car later and smiled and nodded her head.

I read everything I could get my hands on. Any spare money I came by was spent on fishing books. I collected bug samples from the stream and peered at them through a magnifying glass. I began to tie new patterns, some of them more powerful as trout catchers than the ones Gramp had shown me. I learned about egg laying and emergence and spinner falls, water temperature and behavioral drift. All this impressed Jerry and sometimes, when he'd find the time to come along, I'd outfish him. He'd say, "What the hell are you using?" I'd hand him one of my imitations, tell him how to fish it. "What is it?" he'd say. "It's just a fly," I'd say. "I've never seen one like this, where'd you get the idea for it?" I'd shrug my shoulders. "Well, what do you call it?" "Pale Morning Dun," I'd say, and turn so he couldn't see my smile.

But most of the time I was alone. I spent a lot of time sitting on the bank watching the water. That was as important to me now as fishing itself. In all this I felt closer and closer to Gramp, who, it sometimes seemed, was in the trees behind me, watching and smiling. I usually went upstream, though, and did not like going down unless I had to, and then only as far as the pool above Horseman's Run. I could not bring myself to fish Horseman's Run alone.

The meaning of it all, to a mind as young as mine, was a respect for trout I had never found when it mattered how many I caught. Knowing them, their behavior, habits, and needs, made it impossible for me to intentionally harm them. It even seemed unfair to create a pattern that would more easily trick them. Their beauty, bravery, and innocence humbled me. Gramp was right. They were too noble to kill. I had to release every one I caught.

The time came finally to leave. The nearest college was fifty miles away, but I wanted to go to the university with Jerry, and that was another hundred and there were no streams. It was as though that part of my life went on hold while I studied for what I thought then was more important. Judy was there, and it wasn't long before I had a girl. Everything got serious. Everything mattered.

I had never really experienced anything like what I found away from home. The university was old and right in the middle of the city, and they had a brick wall around it. The stuff I'd seen only on television roamed the streets outside. Gangs, drive-by shootings, carjackings, armed robberies. The first week I was there a girl who lived in the dormitory with Judy was raped. A lot of the city people had moved to the suburbs, but apparently that wasn't far enough because, with regularity, somebody got mugged or held up out there where the lawn grew.

I knew even then that it was a matter of time before our small part of the world was discovered by refugees. A few homes had been built before Gramp died. People had moved in from towns as small as Leavitt and Gardiner. What would happen when the suburbs themselves let loose? People wanted land and trees and no burglar alarms or bars on the windows. Who could blame them for envying the safety and beauty I had always known? Though life in the city rewarded initiative, and Jerry found the excitement of being there almost as stimulating as Judy, I was of a different mind. I decided that, when my education was done, I would return home. I knew that what was along the stream where my grandfather had taught me to fish was more important than anything else the world could offer, and though I might not become as prosperous or as famous as Jerry, who had decided to be a big-time trial lawyer, I would make my way, and I would have the stream.

I managed to get home sometimes, on holidays usually, and I always felt guilty when it was time to go. I couldn't fish in the off-season, and I stayed at school to help earn money during the summer. Jerry often wasn't with me anyway, and, worst of all, Gram was slowing down. She sat a lot looking out the window at the hill where Gramp had watched the sunset. She was hard of hearing and did not like asking you to repeat what you said, so she had started talking to herself, always about the past. She didn't talk really, she whispered, just loud enough so you could hear if you were close. Maybe that was because she was hard of hearing to herself as well, I don't know, but I thought of Gramp a lot when I was with her now, stooped and busy with her loneliness.

And then she died.

It was the end of my junior year in the spring with Jerry one term ahead and almost done with pre-law. We went home, and neither of us said much the whole 150 miles. I knew he was going over everything and how, with Gram dead, something had closed and we would truly drift apart.

After the funeral we all sat around remembering, and Mom got out the old pictures. I hadn't seen them since I was a kid and was struck again at how beautiful Gram had been and that Gramp was so tall standing beside her.

"She was the most beautiful woman in the county," Mom said, tapping one of the pictures.

There was Gram in a long white dress and her hair on top of her head and on either side of her, two tall men dressed in suits with high collars. I recognized Gramp. He was thinner, with a long chin.

"Who's the other guy?" I asked.

"Mr. Fario," Mom said.

Jerry and I looked at each other. We stared at the photograph of three people, two of whom were so close and had shared our lives so fully, and this other, who had lurked always around the edges. Mom took the picture of Gram and Gramp and Mr. Fario out of the album and set it on the table.

"He was a fisherman too," she said, "but with bait. He never threw anything back. Finally Gramp would have none of it." She tapped the photo. "I always thought that was so sad." She shook her head. "The place has been sold, you know. A doctor and his wife from Livingston bought it. Want the peace and quiet of the country, I suppose. This whole area will be filled some day, you just watch."

Jerry and I drove out to the old house. Nothing was there, only the frame, floor and roof beams, and the shell of the arch, which hung now over steps that were full of light. The half dead trees were gone. The ground had been plowed and graded. Everything had been cleared from the back. Two men were unloading fresh lumber from a big truck and stacking it to one side. We walked over.

"Well, I guess they saved the shell," I said to one of the men, "but that's not much. We're neighbors."

He shook his head. "It's going too. The interior wood was okay. That's why we took it down piece by piece, and those beams. The old stuff looks good as trim, but it's going right to the ground. They're starting over."

"From the ground up?" I asked.

"Everything," the man said.

We went to the cellar. The door was gone. The heavy concrete steps dropped away, and even now, with the house virtually demolished, the sunlight like a clean, new wave everywhere, at the bottom of the steps was a darkness as profound as night.

"Let's take a look," Jerry said. He put a foot on the first step. I didn't move. "What's the matter?"

I shrugged.

"That's what we always wanted to do, get a peek down there."

"I know."
"Well, come on."
"Jerry, let's go fishing."
"Fishing."
"We haven't gone fishing for a long time."
"You don't want to go down there."
"It's just a hole."
We stood, Jerry with one foot in and me floating helplessly.
Then he said, "Screw it, maybe there's a hatch," and we left.

A letter came at school ten days later, only it wasn't a letter, just an envelope with Mom's handwriting. Inside was a clipping from the *Livingston Herald*. The cellar had been torn up. Beneath layers of concrete they had found the remains of three young boys, neatly in a row. They took Fario out of the cemetery and put him into the ground behind the state penitentiary in Jefferson County.

I did not go home for a long while after that, and I never spoke to Mother about the sons who had been spared in childhood. She never said a word to me.

I went to the river. The water beneath the big oak was gloomy and still, but I knew that, momentarily, light would come and, one by one, miniature sails would appear. To have a chance at life, each pale dun for a time must drift, ignorant of the forms that wait below. That seems to me now eminently fair, and when I too can no longer see the fly, where else would you expect me to be but here, on Horseman's Run, waiting for a rise.

About the Author

Richard Dokey is the author of three story collections and two novels, including *Sanchez and Other Stories, August Heat,* and *The Hollow Man.* He currently resides in Lodi, California.